Walther Ziegler

Schopenhauer
in 60 Minutes

AF187297

Translated by
Alexander Reynolds

My thanks go to Rudolf Aichner for his tireless critical editing; Silke Ruthenberg for the fine graphics; Lydia Pointvogl, Eva Amberger, Christiane Hüttner, and Dr. Martin Engler for their excellent work as manuscript readers and sub-editors; Prof. Guntram Knapp, who first inspired me with enthusiasm for philosophy; and Angela Schumitz, who handled in the most professional manner, as chief editorial reader, the production of both the German and the English editions of this series of books.

My special thanks go to my translator

Dr Alexander Reynolds.

Himself a philosopher, he not only translated the original German text into English with great care and precision but also, in passages where this was required in order to ensure clear understanding, supplemented this text with certain formulations adapted specifically to the needs of English-language readers.

An optimist tells me to open my eyes and look at the world and see how beautiful it is in the sunshine, with its mountains, valleys, plants, animals, rivers and so on. But is the world, then, a peep-show? These things are certainly beautiful to *behold*, but to be them is something quite different.[1]

Bibliographic Information held by the German National Library: The details of the original German edition of this publication are held by the German National Library as part of the German National Bibliography; detailed bibliographical data can be found online at www.dnb.de.

© 2021 Dr Walther Ziegler
1st Edition February 2021
Jacket design and graphic design for the whole book: Silke Ruthenberg, making use of illustrations by:
Raphael Bräsecke, Creactive – Studio for Advertising, Comics & Illustrations
© JackF - Fotolia.com (image-frames)
© Valerie Potapova - Fotolia.com (image-frames)
© Svetlana Gryankina - Fotolia.com (speech-balloons)

Publisher and Printing:
BoD – Books on Demand, Norderstedt
ISBN 9-7837-5049-885-3

Contents

Schopenhauer's Great Discovery

Of all the philosophers, Arthur Schopenhauer (1788-1860) has the reputation of being by far the greatest and most brilliant pessimist. And indeed he did succeed, like no one before him or since, in recognizing, and in describing in gripping, moving language, all the shortcomings, both great and small, of our existences here on earth.

Life on our planet, Schopenhauer argued, has been, since time immemorial, falsely interpreted and portrayed in far too flattering a light. Both philosophers and scientists have assumed, entirely falsely, that Man is *homo sapiens*: a being guided by mind, an *animal rationale*. But this, Schopenhauer goes on, is a great error. Because the fact is that we human beings are not at all guided by reason in the way we live our lives. Rather, we tend to act solely under the impulsion of our deep-lying animal drives:

> Only apparently are people drawn from in front; in reality they are pushed from behind.[2]

We seriously overestimate our own capacities, Schopenhauer insists, already by believing that we can know the world by use of our reason, let alone use reason to guide and direct it. In the first place, he says, we never know the world as it actually is; we only know the idea that we form of it:

> Everyone regards the limits of his field of vision as those of the world [...].[3]

But there is also a second reason and herein lies Schopenhauer's great discovery. Behind all the ideas of the world that we form for ourselves lies a deeper moving principle upon which we never reflect, a kind of primal force inherent in all plants, animals and human beings. This is what Schopenhauer calls "the blind will" or, as he also describes it, "the will-to-live":

Every glance at the world [...] confirms and establishes that the will-to-live [...] is the only true description of the world's innermost nature.[4]

This is the reason why Schopenhauer gave to the great work that was to make him famous the title *The World as Will and Representation*, consciously and deliberately giving pride of place to the notion "will". Because, as he himself says, the core idea of his philosophy can be summed up in a single sentence. Human beings may form for themselves a great mass of different ideas of the world; but in reality the whole world is just the expression of an irrepressible will-to-live which has manifested itself, since the beginning of time, in inanimate matter, in plants, in animals and also in human beings:

> Everything presses and pushes toward existence [...] Let us consider this universal craving for life and see the infinite eagerness, ease and exuberance with which the will-

> to-live presses impetuously into existence under millions of forms everywhere and at every moment by means of fertilizations and germs [...] seizing every opportunity.[5]

The will-to-live is, as Schopenhauer emphasizes here, a "universal craving", that is to say, it is active everywhere and at all times. It is this will-to-live that prompts plants to turn toward the sun and impels animals and human beings to eat, drink and procreate. It operates in the form of the sexual impulse and all other vital impulses, manifesting itself million-fold, at every moment, in every organism on earth.

How deeply this will-to-live permeates our inmost nature can be judged by how frantically any being will resist if the attempt is made to take his life away from him. Regardless of whether the universal will-to-live is manifested, in any given case, in a wasp, a mouse or a human being, the creature permeated and animated by it will in every case struggle, with the same limitless intensity, against death:

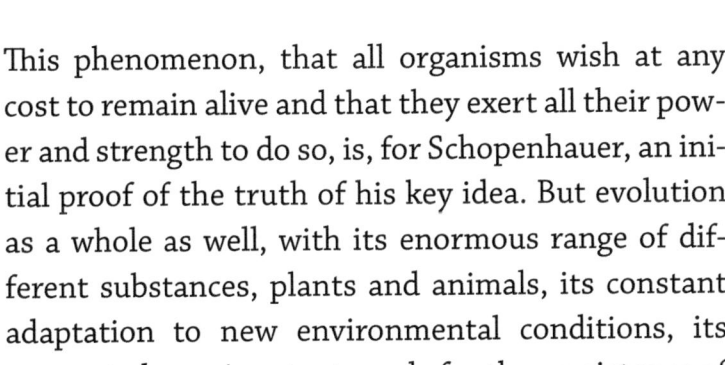

And then again, let us cast a glance at its awful alarm and wild rebellion when in any individual phenomenon it is to pass out of existence [...] The entire inner nature of a living being thus threatened is at once

transformed into the most desperate struggle against, and resistance to, death. Let us see, for example, the terrible anxiety of a person in danger of his life [...] and the boundless rejoicing after he has been saved.[6]

This phenomenon, that all organisms wish at any cost to remain alive and that they exert all their power and strength to do so, is, for Schopenhauer, an initial proof of the truth of his key idea. But evolution as a whole as well, with its enormous range of different substances, plants and animals, its constant adaptation to new environmental conditions, its protracted, passionate struggle for the persistence of certain species, seems to Schopenhauer to be a sure indication of the universal operation of the so-called "blind will" to live:

Everything presses and pushes toward existence, if possible toward *organic* existence [...] In animal nature it then becomes obvious that *will-to-live* is the keynote of its being, its only unchangeable and unconditioned quality.[7]

The will, then, is the only "unchangeable keynote" of our being. The notion, cherished for thousands of years by both theologians and philosophers, that it is Reason, be it human or divine, that is the really determining moment behind all living things is, Schopenhauer insists, in the end a completely untenable notion:

Instead of this, it is the blind will, appearing as the tendency to life, the love of life, vital energy; it is the same thing as makes the plant grow.[8]

But why does Schopenhauer speak of a *blind will*? Does this will-to-live not have a goal and a purpose: namely, as he himself admits, the preservation of the species?

> But on closer consideration we shall find here also that it is rather a blind urge, an impulse wholly without ground or motive.[9]

Looked at closely, then, the will-to-live is a "blind urge without motive" because, in the end, it pursues no recognizable or even meaningful goal:

> But what is the ultimate aim of it all? To sustain ephemeral and harassed individuals through a short span of time, in the most fortunate case with endurable want [...].

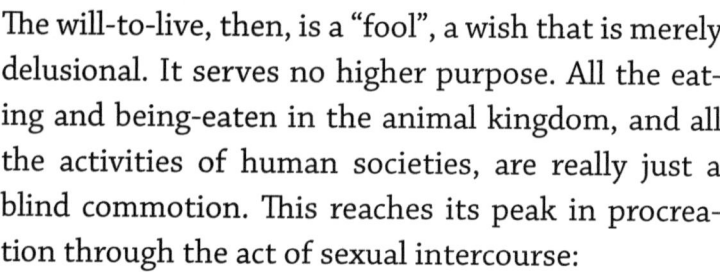

Then the propagation of this race and of its activities. With this evident want of proportion between the effort and the reward the will-to-live, taken objectively, appears to us from this point of view as a fool, or

taken subjectively, as a delusion. Seized by this, every living thing works with the utmost exertion of its strength for something which has no value.[10]

The will-to-live, then, is a "fool", a wish that is merely delusional. It serves no higher purpose. All the eating and being-eaten in the animal kingdom, and all the activities of human societies, are really just a blind commotion. This reaches its peak in procreation through the act of sexual intercourse:

Nature, the inner essence of which is the will-to-live itself, drives with all its force the human being, just as it does the animal, to procreate.[11]

The "intensity of the urge" here leads inevitably to an uncontrolled increase in population, to terrible wars, and eventually to

[...] over-population of the entire planet, the terrible evil of which only a bold imagination can conjure up in the mind.[12]

But the will-to-live is blind above all because, generally speaking, it cannot know or reflect upon itself. This lack of self-knowledge comes to expression when it enters into the different individuals who make up the human race and manifests itself with an equal intensity at the same time in every one of these mutually contending individuals. Schopenhauer explicitly states that the will-to-live "individuates itself" but neither becomes, through this individuation, less intense nor really has to divide itself up. It continues to operate in each individual with the same absolute, indivisible energy. It is just herein that it shows its unreflecting "foolishness". Because one and the same will-to-live that drives on the hungry wolf to hunt and kill the deer drives on, at the same time, the deer to try to escape the jaws of the wolf. This means that the will

[…] seeking enhanced wellbeing in *one* of its phenomena (i.e. the wolf) produces great suffering in *another* (i.e. the deer). In the fierceness and

intensity of its desire it buries its teeth in its own flesh, not knowing that it always injures only itself […].[13]

In other words

Tormentor and tormented are one.[14]

The "blind" will neither notices that it is, in this way, brutally cannibalizing itself nor would it care if it did so notice. It is a force without morality, self-reflection, or self-control.

[...] The will is originally and in itself without knowledge and blind.[15]

Not even the much-vaunted sovereign, majestic placidity and beauty of the lion should delude us as to the fact that he too owes his existence to this blind, brutal urge alone and stands, as it were, atop a mountain of corpses, by whose blood he has bought this existence, which will last only until he himself falls victim to this cannibalistic will. The same stubborn will, indeed, as inheres in the lion inheres also in the humble weeds that, once torn out, immediately begin to grow back again:

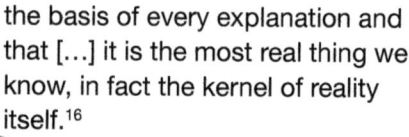

Therefore in such phenomena it becomes evident that I have rightly declared the will-to-live to be that which is incapable of further explanation but is

the basis of every explanation and that [...] it is the most real thing we know, in fact the kernel of reality itself.[16]

The will, then, is that kernel of all reality which is not susceptible of any further explanation. It is also, as Schopenhauer also describes it, "metaphysical". What does this mean? The word "metaphysical" is formed from two Ancient Greek words *meta* and *physis*. To say that the will is "metaphysical" signifies that it extends back behind, or alternatively that it extends beyond, all that is merely physical. What this signifies, then, is that the will-to-live is not a drive that can be perceived by the physical senses, nor any natural phenomenon or natural law that can be measured using the tools of science. Rather, it is that force which underlies all measurements and scientific determinations and which alone makes them possible. Because in contrast to its individual manifestations, running from the amoeba through the dinosaurs right up to all the individual forms of existence today, the will-to-live is an eternal force which remains always absolutely constant and which forms the background and basis for everything:

The will alone is unchangeable and simply identical.[17]

Thus far, then, Schopenhauer's key philosophical idea is easy to grasp and follow. We must all surely agree, he argues, that we ourselves and all the organisms that we find around us wish to go on living. In other words, it must be conceded, firstly, that there is such a thing as a "will-to-live" and, secondly, that just such a will needs to cannibalize itself if it is to persist in its existence. In this way, the will in question inevitably causes pain and suffering:

> [...] Let us merely look at it, this world of constantly needy creatures who continue for a time merely by devouring one another, pass their existence in anxiety and want, and often endure terrible afflictions, until at last they fall into the arms of death.[18]

This mutual inflicting of pain does not apply to the animal kingdom alone. Human beings too, Schopenhauer points out, have, since the beginning of time, enslaved, exploited, martyred and murdered one another. In this regard, indeed, we are considerably worse than animals, inasmuch as we use our reason to pursue such activities and oppress, for example, all other species, turning them into factory products. The basic pattern of behaviour for human beings is egoism, which makes it inevitable that we become entangled in a "war of all against all":

> The world is just a hell, and in it human beings are the tortured souls on the one hand and the devils on the other.[19]

Over and over again Schopenhauer draws for us, as no other philosopher before or since has done, a deeply sombre portrait of human existence and of the path that we are all bound to follow, from our conception by our parents in the sensually pleasurable act of sexual intercourse down to a miserable sickening and death in our old age:

What a difference there is, indeed, between our beginning and our end. The former in the frenzy of desire and the ecstasy of sensual pleasure, the latter in the destruction of all organs and the musty odour of corpses. The path between these two also goes

steadily downhill with respect to wellbeing and enjoying life. Blissfully dreaming childhood, joyful youth,

toilsome manhood, frail, often pitiful old age, the torments of final illness and finally the agony of death. Does it not look exactly as if existence were a blunder whose consequences gradually become more and more obvious? [20]

Schopenhauer answers this last question with a re-sounding "yes". Life, in the last analysis, is a mistake, a kind of accident of evolution, something deeply unpleasant that the universe has unreasonably imposed upon us. Because this blind will that is the driving force behind all that occurs on our planet serves only to cause lifelong suffering to every living being:

If we picture to ourselves roughly, as far as we can, the sum total of misery, pain and suffering of every kind on which the sun shines in its course, we shall admit that it would

have been much better if it had been just as impossible for the sun to produce the phenomenon of life on earth as on the moon [...].[21]

It would have been better, then, Schopenhauer believes, if no form of life had ever arisen on the earth at all. Because, as Schopenhauer declares in summary of his whole philosophical position, we must surely all of us recognize

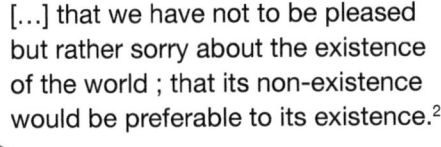

[...] that we have not to be pleased but rather sorry about the existence of the world ; that its non-existence would be preferable to its existence.[22]

This radical conclusion that it would be better not to live, indeed best to have never been born at all, earned Schopenhauer the reputation of being the greatest pessimist and misanthrope of all time. And indeed Schopenhauer did tend to avoid, in his daily life, large parties and gatherings. He remained a life-long bachelor, living in rented accommodation and pursuing the solitary profession of "private scholar". Only for a very brief period did he try to assume a more public role as an intellectual, taking on the job of lecturer at the recently-founded University of Berlin. Deliberately and provocatively, however, he insisted that his lectures be scheduled at exactly the same hour on the same day as the lectures of the far more famous Hegel. When, understandably, almost no students chose him over the renowned teacher known at the time as the "philosophical dictator of

Germany", he forswore, in disgust, all further participation in university life.

Thanks to a small inheritance from his father, who had died at an early age, Schopenhauer was able to lead a simple but independent life without having, as he put it, to "twist, turn, accommodate and renounce his convictions"[23] in the way that philosophy professors dependent on the university for their salary were forced to do.

Throughout most of his life, then, Schopenhauer barely left his sparsely-furnished two-room apartment except to eat in a restaurant or take his dog "Atma" for lengthy walks. He called this beloved pet "Atma" in reference to the Vedantic philosophical name for "the World-Soul".[24] But when "Atma"'s behaviour annoyed him, he called him "Man"!

One other very characteristic scene from Schopenhauer's life, often foregrounded by his biographers, concerned the common space that he had, due to the very modest circumstances in which he lived, to share with his neighbour, a certain seamstress in her forties by the name of Caroline Marquet. On one occasion this woman was conversing so loudly and persistently with some female friends in close proximity to Schopenhauer's study that, failing to persuade her to desist, the philosopher cursed her and pushed her out into the stairwell area where, according to her own account, she fell down and injured her arm, resulting in a persisting nervous trembling of this limb. She brought criminal charges against Schopenhauer and the philosopher was sentenced by a court to pay out to Miss Marquet "compensation for personal suffering" in the amount of 60 talers annually, to continue until this trembling ceased. Schopenhauer could not help retorting to the judge who imposed this penalty that Miss Marquet would surely be clever enough to ensure that the "trembling of the arm" in question went on all her life. Time proved him right. The notoriously tight-fisted Schopenhauer ended up paying this "compensation for personal suffering" to Miss Marquet for no less than twenty-seven years. When he finally received in the post notification of the old woman's death and a copy of her death certificate, he scribbled on this latter:

Obit anus, abit onus (The old one dies, the burden goes away).[25]

Such anecdotes, as well as the inarguably radically pessimistic nature of his philosophy, have given rise to a picture of Schopenhauer as a cantankerous hermit who most likely developed only in the course of a long life this ever deeper mistrust toward his fellow human beings. But this picture is misleading. Astonishingly, Schopenhauer arrived already as a young man at this deeply sceptical view of the world and of Man:

In my seventeenth year, without any learned school education, I was affected by the wretchedness of life, as was the Buddha when, in his youth, he caught sight of sickness, old age, pain and death [...] The result for me was that this world could not be the work of an all-good being but rather that of a devil [...].[26]

Already as a young man of twenty-three he had said to the old German poet Wieland:

> Life is a troublesome affair and I have resolved to spend my own life reflecting on it.[27]

He had completed, indeed, his masterpiece, *The World as Will and Representation*, already before he was thirty years old, an achievement almost unique in the history of philosophy. His pessimistic assessment of life and the world was, then, clearly something that arose very early in his experience. When, at the age of 16, he visited the French harbour city of Toulon with his parents, certain old galleys were still being used as prisons, with the prisoners chained to benches like the galley-slaves of ancient times. Schopenhauer was deeply impressed with the persistent will-to-live of men in such awful positions:

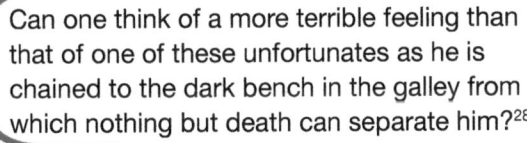

> Can one think of a more terrible feeling than that of one of these unfortunates as he is chained to the dark bench in the galley from which nothing but death can separate him?[28]

Of still greater significance for his philosophy than such experiences, however, was, we may imagine, Schopenhauer's difficult relationship with his mother. Johanna Schopenhauer was a successful novelist in these very early years of the 19th century and after the early death of her husband, which may have been a case either of accident or of suicide, she moved with her son to the great cultural centre of Weimar. The "salon" that she created there was frequented by such luminaries of the German intellectual life of the time as Wieland, the Schlegel brothers and even the great Goethe himself. Johanna was a believer in "free love" and led a very lively sex-life for the time.

Schopenhauer often criticized his mother on this account. But the real quarrels between them were not due to this but rather due to the deeply pessimistic opinions with which the young Arthur had the habit of driving away the guests of his mother's "salon". We find his mother writing to him on one occasion: "You are not without intellect and education [...] but you are nevertheless irritating and unbearable and I consider it most difficult to live with you [...] because of your rage at wanting to know everything better than others. With this, you embitter the people around you [...]"[29] In the end, Johanna Schopenhauer disinherited her son, cutting off contact with him entirely.

Whether, and to what extent, this difficult relationship affected the young Schopenhauer also in his philosophical meditations must, in the end, remain a matter of speculation. What is certain is that he saw, from very early on, human life from an incorruptibly dark and sober perspective. His core philosophical notion was clear and simple. We are constantly impelled through our existence by the will-to-live and this will, by creating needs, thereby also creates suffering. Much like the Buddhists whose work he was one of the first in Europe to closely study, Schopenhauer concludes: "To live is to suffer":

The story of every life is thus a story of suffering.[30]

But Schopenhauer does not leave things here. He would not, indeed, have been a philosopher if he had not drawn certain specific conclusions from this recognition of the terrible facts. We must first, he argued, accept the world and our own inner nature for what they are: namely, blind will. But this acceptance alone produces a first small improvement in our situation. If we recognize and accept for what it is the blind impelled-ness that makes up most of what we call human life, we can take a calmer and more patient attitude to all the things that might otherwise seem infuriating and provocative. Having accepted this, we begin intuitively to sense and to understand that other human beings too are similarly impelled, and victims of one and the same blind will-to-live as ourselves. This means that we can begin also to identify with their situation and with their suffering. This capacity for identification with others, which is commonly known as "pity", can, when translated into the active giving of help, and selfless action for others' sake, even liberate us, even if only for short periods, from the egoism otherwise imposed on us by the blind urge to live and flourish.

We can even, Schopenhauer continues, take yet another step beyond this. We can say "no" to life. By "saying 'no' to life" he does not mean committing suicide but rather only performing a negation of the "blind will". We can, Schopenhauer believes, succeed in refusing our basic state of "impelled-ness" through such means as art, ascetic exercises, or meditation:

Man attains to the state of voluntary renunciation, resignation, true composure, and complete willlessness [...] the negation of the will-to-live.[31]

But what does this mean, concretely? How is it possible for me to say "no" to life? What does it mean to live "ascetically"? If our life is nothing other than a realization of blind will, a senseless eating and being-eaten, how is it possible to escape from this cycle at all? Can we really be freed from it simply by ascetic exercises? And also: of what use to us is Schopenhauer's pessimism in the present day? Do we not rather find recommended to us today, by everyone and everywhere, optimism and "positive thinking"? Schopenhauer provides us with fascinating, uncompromising answers to all these questions.

Schopenhauer's Central Idea

The World is Only My Representation

Schopenhauer's main work and masterpiece, *The World as Will and Representation*, begins with a very short, simple sentence:

"The world is my representation" [...].[32]

But already this apparently simple statement of fact contains a provocation. If the whole world is only "my representation", this means that I may well not be seeing the world as it is at all but rather only as I imagine it to be. But this is indeed what Schopenhauer is claiming by advancing this proposition. All the things that we take to be real and objective we owe in fact only to our ideas or images of these things:

For that the objective existence of things is conditioned by a represented of them, and that consequently the objective world exists only as a representation, is no hypothesis [...] On the contrary, it is the surest and simplest truth [...].[33]

In the first instance, then, the world consists only of the ideas or representations that we have of it. Thus, the lumberjack whose job it is to cut down a tall tree will certainly have a different "representation" of this tree in his mind than will the children who like to climb on it, or than the courting couple who come there in the evening to kiss and cuddle under its boughs. One and the same tree, one and the same world, are perceived in very different ways:

Each carries within himself, as his representation, the single world that he is really acquainted with [...].[34]

This is the reason why we often find ourselves "talking past one another" and saying to one another things like "what strange ideas you have" or "my goodness, what kind of a world do you think you're living in?" Schopenhauer draws a very serious conclusion from such apparently trivial turns of phrase:

Even if they are in the same environment, every human being lives in a different world. Since everything that exists for a person exists always

only in their consciousness [...] what is surely, at least in the first instance, decisive is: how this consciousness is made.[35]

But how is our consciousness made? How exactly does it function? Schopenhauer relies, in his philosophy of knowledge and perception, very strongly on Immanuel Kant, for whose writings he had an enormous admiration. Already several decades before Schopenhauer Kant had proven that we human beings perceive and know the world only through not just one but two types of "filter": firstly, through our necessary sorting of all that we perceive into the forms of time and space; and secondly through the further organization of these perceptions in terms of the "categories of thought". Our minds are so made, Kant argued, that we are compelled first to order everything that we encounter in terms of its place in the sequence of time and its position vis-à-vis other things in the order of space and then to further order these things located in time and space in terms of logical inter-relations, such as one being the cause of, or caused by, another. In other words, whether we wish to or not, we are simply made in such a way that the world must present itself to us as composed of things that "exist now", "will exist later", or that "happened before" or "happened long ago". We are also made in such a way that all that we encounter must present itself to us as "next to", "behind", or "above" other things and so on. And finally, our minds are so made that whatever enters our field of knowledge must do so in a form that concords with certain logical dimensions or classes. Any known tree, for example, will have to fall into such categories as "wooden", "big", "heavy", "green", or "about to fall over" and furthermore into such logical relations as "about to fall over *because* the lumberjack has cut deeply into its trunk with his axe." Kant also strongly emphasized, however, that, given these "filters" placed before all our knowledge, it is impossible for us to know anything about how the world might look if these filters were not there. The "thing in it-self", the "tree in itself", the "world in itself" remain secrets for us. All we can know of them is that there must be "something" there for our minds to "filter".

But it is just at this point that Schopenhauer goes beyond, and contradicts, his admired philosophical master Kant:

> Man carries the ultimate fundamental secrets within himself and this fact is accessible to him in the most immediate way.[36]

Man has, Schopenhauer insists, not only a representation of the world around him but also of himself and his living body. And it is just this living body that necessarily alerts us to the fact that there does exist, behind all our conscious representations of the world, something specific and knowable: namely, that universal will that is the will-to-live. Contrary, then, to what Kant believed, we can acquire knowledge even of the inmost essence of the world and of the things that make it up. Our living body unlocks for us what Kant considers to be the impenetrable "secret" that is the "world in itself". This is the case inasmuch as, in contrast to the way in which we represent to ourselves everything else in the world, we have, of our own bodies, a double representation or experience:

(The body) is given in intelligent perception, as representation, as an object among objects [...] But it is also given in quite a different way, namely as [...] will.[37]

In other words, we perceive our own body, and represent it to ourselves, in the first place just as we would perceive and represent to ourselves a wardrobe or a chair: i.e. as an object of a specific height and weight. Above and beyond this, however, we also perceive and experience our bodily existence in a much more intense and direct way that has nothing to do with the way we experience the wardrobe or the chair. We experience ourselves through our bodies as beings impelled by drives and urges, such as hunger, thirst, sexual desire and needs of many other kinds. In other words, we experience ourselves through our bodies as beings consisting of will:

> Everyone finds himself to be this will, in which the inner nature of the world consists.[38]

Once we have discovered in this way, in a first step, the will within ourselves in the form of an individual certainty of its presence, we can then go on, in a second step, to discover the reality and operation of this will in the entirety of external Nature:

> (Whoever) with me has gained this conviction will find that of itself it will become the key to the knowledge of the innermost being of the whole of Nature,

> since he now transfers it to all those phenomena that are given to him not, like his own phenomenon, in both direct and indirect knowledge, but in the latter solely [...].[39]

By transferring, then, our direct certainty of our own existence as will onto other human beings, animals and, in the end, onto the whole of Nature, we recognize will-to-live to be the force that pervades and constitutes the universe as a whole:

My whole philosophy can be summed up in one expression: the world is the self-knowledge of the will.[40]

The Real World as Blind Will

For Schopenhauer, then, there lies behind all the phenomena that make up the world and even, interestingly, behind the forces and motions involved in the non-organic part of Nature, a single universal, indivisible, eternal Will. Every human being, he argues, should be able to come in the end to recognize

[...] the force that turns the magnet to the North Pole, [...] yes, even gravitation, which acts so powerfully in all matter, pulling the stone to the earth and the

earth to the sun, [...] as that which is immediately known to him so intimately and better than everything else and which, where it appears most distinctly, is called *will*.[41]

The world, indeed, may initially appear, due to the many different representations that we form of it, to be an extremely variegated thing that is, moreover, entirely alien in its nature to us who live in it. Where we examine it closely, however, we find it indeed to consist always and only of that very same underlying urge or drive as we feel, directly and immediately, operating in our own selves. This urge or drive, Schopenhauer argues, can be discovered to be at work already in the physical processes occurring in the inanimate, inorganic parts of Nature (i.e. minerals, atmospheric forces etc). One step up the scale to sentience, in the plant world, the operation of this drive is even clearer. Once one directs one's attention to the world of sentient animal life, however, it is completely unmistakable:

> In animal Nature it then becomes obvious that will-to-live is the keynote of its being, its only unchangeable and unconditioned quality.[42]

We human beings may, indeed, walk upright and thus present a different outward form from the other animals, and there may also exist significant character differences between one member of the human race and another. But the same clock is ticking within us all. Considered from Schopenhauer's viewpoint, we are just puppets in a giant world-theatre. Our strings are pulled, however, not by some agent external to us, such as God or some God-like cosmic puppet-master, but we are rather set and kept in motion by this "clockwork" internal to us all:

> Therefore I have said that these puppets are not pulled from outside but that each of them bears in itself the clockwork from which its movements result. This is the *will-to-live* [...].[43]

One and the same clockwork of the will-to-live ticks on in the human being, the magnet, the plant and the whole variety of animals:

Like every other part of Nature, Man is objectivity of the will [...].[44]

In the course of the many millennia of Man's evolution this will has given external form, in the various human organs, to its inner nature and the aspects of its blind drive:

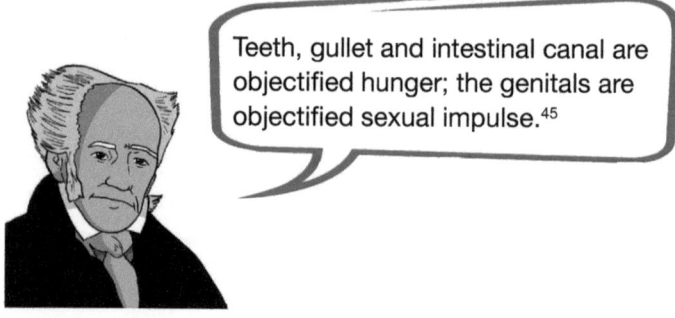

Teeth, gullet and intestinal canal are objectified hunger; the genitals are objectified sexual impulse.[45]

But there is, in Schopenhauer's view, after all one unique quality, or at least one gradual difference from other beings, which tends to set Man off, from a certain point in his development onward, from all other component elements of Nature. This is the emergence in Man, very late in the history of the planet, of the capacity for self-awareness, or self-consciousness. Because, in distinction from the phenomena of the physical world, from plants and even from other animals, Man is able to recognize and think about the "clockwork" that is driving him on, even as it continues to do so:

Man is the most complete phenomenon of the will [...] Therefore in Man the will can reach full self-consciousness.[46]

But this self-consciousness that the will attains in Man, and this clear recognition that we are all being driven on by a blind instinctive force, is not something that frees us from this force or radically alters the lives of us human beings. The "clockwork" does indeed continue to drive us on even as we come to know and recognize it. Even despite this achieved self-awareness, we must continue to do much as the un-self-aware animals do: eat, drink and follow the restless urge to procreate. Because consciousness, in the end, is no liberator but rather only a servant: a kind of tool that is used by the will in order to more skilfully satisfy its drives and urges:

The will [...] brought forth consciousness for its own purposes.[47]

Our consciousness, then, or in other words our capacity for reason and understanding, is merely something secondary. The will has created this capacity for thought and reasoning the better to achieve its own irrational ends. For this reason Schopenhauer describes our power of reason as something that is employed by the will just as the blacksmith employs a hammer, i.e. as a useful tool. Thus, our reason and understanding come into play above all once the lower drives have awakened and fixated on something they desire:

The understanding of the stupidest person becomes keen when it is a question of (acquiring) objects that closely concern his willing.[48]

Intellect, then, is something ancillary that was not to be found anywhere in Nature until the will found it had an interest in creating it:

But with this expedient [...] *the world as representation* now stands out at one stroke with all its forms [...] The world now shows its second side; hitherto mere will, it is now at the same time *representation* [...].[49]

This "expedient" of intellect served, indeed, in many minor and less minor practical matters, to aid Man in achieving his ends and aims. He could now go about his hunting more cleverly and calculatingly, setting traps, for example, for the animals he wanted to kill. He could also build houses and bridges. But, considered in the larger and longer term, the birth of intellect was also a burden on human existence because now, suddenly, Man was able to form a conception of his own death:

45

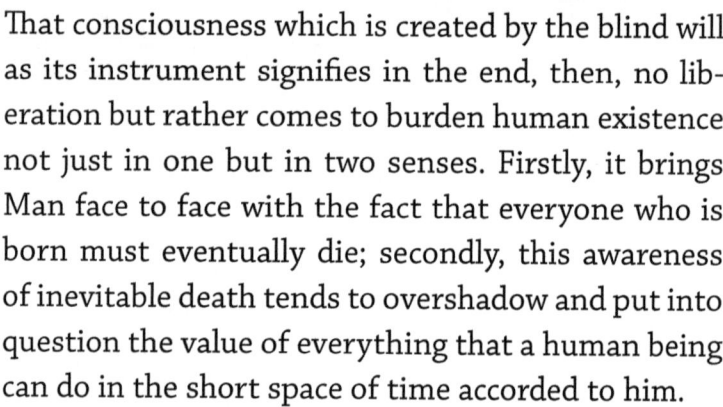

No beings, with the exception of Man, feel surprised at their own existence [...] (And Man's surprise) is all the more serious as here,

for the first time, (the will) stands consciously face to face with death and, besides the finiteness of all existence, the vanity and fruitlessness of all effort forces themselves on it [...].[50]

That consciousness which is created by the blind will as its instrument signifies in the end, then, no liberation but rather comes to burden human existence not just in one but in two senses. Firstly, it brings Man face to face with the fact that everyone who is born must eventually die; secondly, this awareness of inevitable death tends to overshadow and put into question the value of everything that a human being can do in the short space of time accorded to him.

The Sixfold Suffering Caused by the Blind Will-to-Live

In fact, the blind will-to-live condemns human beings not just to these two forms of suffering, death and the sense of meaninglessness caused by knowing one will die, but to what might be itemised as six forms of suffering in total. **Firstly** we suffer through our own basic bodily needs. Hunger, thirst and sexual desires are experienced by us, Schopenhauer argues, as "lacks". When we are thirsty, for example, this is a suffering that signals to us that the body lacks liquids:

All willing springs from lack, from deficiency, and thus from suffering. Fulfilment brings this to an end; but for every one wish that is fulfilled there are at least ten that are denied [...].[51]

But even if we could, for the space of a moment, have all our wishes and needs fulfilled, we suffer **secondly** from the constant recurrence of these needs. Every meal, every act of sexual intercourse, affords us only a brief "pause to catch our breath", a satisfaction lasting just an hour or a day at most, before the same needs and drives make themselves felt once again:

[...] The wish fulfilled at once makes way for a new one [...] No attained object of willing can give a satisfaction that lasts and no longer declines; but it is always like the alms thrown to a beggar, which reprieves him today so that his misery may be prolonged till tomorrow.[52]

The blind will-to-live, then, condemns us to a constant longing, a constant restlessness and disquiet:

[...] We never obtain lasting happiness or peace. [...] The subject of willing is [...] constantly drawing water in the sieve of the Danaids [...].[53]

This image of "the sieve of the Danaids" is one which Schopenhauer drew from classical mythology. According to the ancient myth, the fifty daughters of King Danaus all murdered their husbands on their wedding nights and were condemned, therefore, by

Zeus to spending eternity in Hades carrying water to a pot not in buckets but in sieves, so that, each time they reached their goal, they no longer had any water in their receptacle and had to go back and begin all over again. The blind will, suggests Schopenhauer, is like this "sieve of the Danaids", because it demands constantly to be "filled" with some form of satisfaction but is always "empty" again, and demanding to be "filled" once more, within moments of "satisfaction"'s being accorded it.

Here, indeed, one might raise an objection and ask: "Is it not rather a good thing that hunger, thirst and sexual desire recur again and again? Does this not ensure that human beings likewise again and again experience the pleasure of satisfying these needs and desires?" But Schopenhauer repudiates this objection extremely vehemently:

Whoever wants summarily to test the assertion that the pleasure in the world outweighs the pain, or at any rate that the two balance each other, should compare the feelings of an animal that is devouring another with those of that other.[54]

Thirdly, we suffer from the fact of the blind will-to-live's having "individuated itself" into the great plurality of individual living beings. Because, having been "individuated" in this way, these many separate organisms necessarily end up becoming involved in a constant existential struggle with one another, a "war of all against all":

> Thus everywhere in Nature we see contest, struggle and the fluctuation of victory and [...] recognize in this [...] that variance with itself essential to the will. Every grade of the will's objectification fights for the matter, the space, and the time of another.[55]

This, the will's fighting for "matter, space and time" goes on constantly between the millions of plants, animals and human beings into which it has "individuated itself". Plants which grow up too closely together "fight for space" in the sense that one tends to block the sunlight from another, until the latter withers and dies. Animals, in their turn, consume plants, and also other animals, in order to maintain themselves. But the most brutal fight of all is conducted by Man, who has subjugated the whole of Nature and turned much of it into a kind of factory commodity. Man raises plants and vegetables in such artificial constructions as greenhouses and shuts up living animals in pens and stalls:

Thus, the will-to-live generally feasts on itself, and is in different forms its own nourishment, until finally the human race, because it subdues all the others, regards

Nature as manufactured for its own use. [...] (But) this same human race reveals in itself with terrible clearness that conflict, that variance of the will with itself and we get *homo homini lupus.*[56]

Schopenhauer alludes here to the famous saying of the British philosopher Thomas Hobbes: "Man is a wolf to Man". Because, in Schopenhauer's observation as in Hobbes's, human beings had been involved, throughout the whole of history, as nations and collectives in struggles for fertile land and territory but also as individuals with one another for their private gains and advantages. Schopenhauer could look back, for evidence of this, to all the wars of the past and also to such recently-abolished practices as slavery; but he saw sufficient evidence, indeed, in the social realities of his own day, such as the mass exploitation of Man by Man in the factories of 19th-century Europe, where men, women and even children were obliged to "perform the same mechanical work" for ten, twelve or fourteen hours a day for almost no money:

But this is the fate of millions [...].[57]

Since all living beings are dependent on the basic metabolic processes, such as breathing, eating and drinking, and need constantly to be appropriating whatever is needed for these processes to continue, there is simply no way out of that mutual cannibalism that is the basic structure of our universe. Everything devours everything else:

At bottom, this springs from the fact that the will must live on itself, since nothing exists beside it, and it is a hungry will. Hence arise pursuit, hunting, anxiety and suffering.[58]

Schopenhauer provides us with a whole series of striking and gruesome examples of how this "hungry will" manifests itself on our planet. He describes, for example, certain kinds of spider in whom the female of the species devours the male after this latter has fertilized her eggs; or insects that project their eggs into members of other insect species, so that the emerging larvae eat their way out of their hosts in order to be born. He also writes of giant turtles which, coming up onto land from the sea to lay their eggs,

[...] are seized by wild dogs (who), with their united strength [...], lay them on their backs, tear open their lower armour, the small scales of the belly, and devour them alive [...].

All this misery is repeated thousands and thousands of times, year in, year out. For this, then, are these turtles born.[59]

But perhaps the most impressive example of the "self-individuation" of the blind and "hungry" will, and of the cruel struggle that it gives rise to, is given by Schopenhauer in the form of his description of the bulldog-ant:

[...] The most glaring example of this kind is afforded by the bulldog-ant of Australia, for when it is cut in two a battle begins between the head and the tail. The head

attacks the tail with its teeth and the tail defends itself bravely by stinging the head. The contest usually lasts for half an hour, until they die or are dragged away by other ants. This takes place every time.[60]

Schopenhauer cites, in fact, a large number of natural phenomena and events which seem to bear witness to the fact that the will-to-live, once it has "individuated" itself into some singular form or figure of life, begins immediately to assert itself in this form of life in the most blind and ruthless way. Indeed, in the just-cited case of the ant cut in two, the will-to-live continues to stage its egotistical struggle even between two halves of a being which had formerly been just one. We observe, it is true, in both human and animal communities certain forms of essentially social behaviour, such as the collective parenting behaviour known as "brood care".

[...] But in general [...] the world is in a very bad way. In savage countries they eat one another; in civilized countries they deceive one another. And that is what people call the way of the world![61]

The **fourth** major dimension of suffering to which the will-to-live condemns human beings is worry and anxiety about the future. This suffering is indeed peculiar to human beings, since neither plants nor even animals know such things as fear of hardship in old age or worry about other threats which might emerge only in the future:

> The animal is the embodiment of the present [...] It is just this complete absorption in the present moment [...] which contributes so much to the pleasure we derive from our domestic pets.[62]

If an animal has had its fill of eating and drinking, it will simply sit there radiating peace and contentment. A human being, on the other hand, will, even with a full belly, be worrying about where tomorrow's meal is coming from. A human being will tend also always to have one principal care or worry that weighs on him quite especially, be it an unfulfilled wish or an anxiety regarding poverty or sickness:

> [...] If a great and pressing care is finally lifted from our breast by a fortunate issue, another immediately takes its place [...].[63]

And even if the matter that is causing care and anxiety in this new case is, when considered soberly and objectively, much more trivial than the care one has just been relieved of

[...] It knows how to blow itself out, so that it apparently equals (the former care) in size and thus, as the chief care of the day, completely fills the throne.[64]

This fact, then, that Man always worries about the future and that every source of care and worry, even when "dethroned" by a solution, will always see some other immediately "take its throne" is the fourth major form of suffering for human beings in this world. The **fifth** major dimension of suffering, however, is, remarkably, one which tends to arise precisely at times when a person is not beset by any care or worry. The head of a family may, for example, have arrived in a position of such wealth and power that he can see to all the needs and wishes of himself, his wife and all his children for all the foreseeable future. Just at this point, however, he is likely to be afflicted by a new form of suffering: namely, boredom. The danger in boredom consists in the fact that one's energies are no longer occupied. Existence no longer has any concrete goal set for it and is driven back upon itself. Where there had previously been an agitated round of problems to deal with and solve, there now arises an uncanny rest and stillness. Time seems no longer to be passing at all.

We become conscious of time when we are bored, not when we are amused. Both cases prove that our existence is happiest when we perceive it least. From this it follows that it would be better not to have it at all.[65]

Human existence here makes the painful discovery that the only "meaning of life" consists in the strenuous, wearisome maintaining of life itself and that, once this strain is removed, it has no "meaning" at all:

Behind need and want is to be found, at once, boredom, which attacks even the more intelligent animals. This is a consequence of the fact that life has no *genuine intrinsic worth* [...].[66]

Schopenhauer's observation here regarding "the more intelligent animals" is quite correct. It does indeed often occur that animals kept in a zoo, who no longer have to see to their own day-to-day survival, become neurotic or apathetic. For similar reasons, human beings often fear the day on which they will reach an age where they no longer have to go to work every day. Some, indeed, begin to feel this panic in the face of "free time" long before the age of retirement and try to make sure, by filling their daily schedules with every sort of social engagement above and beyond their professional ones, that they never have to feel threatened by boredom at all:

[...] But as soon as this comes to a standstill, the utter barrenness and emptiness of existence become apparent.[67]

The suffering involved in this experience of "the utter barrenness and emptiness of existence" is, for Schopenhauer, yet another indication that life, just in itself, has no value and is something that is driven on just by a blind will-to-live:

If life [...] had a positive value and in itself a real intrinsic worth, there could not possibly be any boredom.[68]

There is, then, simply no way out of suffering because we are always either vainly pursuing the satisfaction of our needs or, where we do indeed succeed in satisfying them, we fall victim to the pain of boredom:

Life swings like a pendulum to and fro between pain and boredom.[69]

Not even those "joys of love" so often lauded by the poets offer any real relief here. Love itself, argues Schopenhauer, is merely a promising illusion:

For all amorousness is rooted in the sexual impulse alone [...], however ethereally (delicately) it may deport itself.[70]

And the sexual impulse, in its turn, serves primarily the purpose of preserving the species. This same impulse, indeed, drives men to marry. But the women they marry, claims Schopenhauer, lose their sexual charms, at the very latest, after having borne one or two children, so that very soon the illusion of love evaporates:

> In this way (the sexual impulse) becomes for (the man in question) a source of much suffering and little pleasure.[71]

Marriage, however, is just a small additional farce added to the great tragi-comedy of life. The **sixth**, and perhaps the greatest, of the sufferings that existence imposes upon us is death, and thereby the fact that

> The life of our body (is) only a constantly-prevented dying, an ever-deferred death.[72]

Thus, every action that we take becomes questionable. Whatever we do or succeed in achieving, we are always living, so to speak, "on credit" and this "credit", that the time allotted to our lives surely is, is melting away day by day:

> Every evening we are poorer by a day.[73]

While we are children we do not feel this burden. In these very early years of our lives we sit, as it were, in front of a great stage-curtain in the theatre and wait impatiently, full of joyful anticipation, to see what will emerge into our sight and experience once it is drawn back:

It is a blessing that we do not know what will actually come.[74]

Even in the early years of adulthood we are generally able to push the notion of death entirely out of our immediate consciousness:

The cheerfulness and buoyancy of our youth are due partly to the fact that we are climbing the hill of life and do not see death that lies at the foot of the other side.[75]

But already in our thirty-sixth year, claims Schopenhauer, we cross the "summit" of this hill and are from then on able to perceive more and more clearly just what is waiting for us "at the foot of the other side". In his typically highly imagistic language, Schopenhauer also compares human beings and their life-plans with ships whose crews, full of hope, set sail for the open sea in the expectation of discovering new countries and thereby acquiring power, fame and honour:

> As a rule, everyone ultimately reaches port with masts and rigging gone; but then it is immaterial whether he was happy or unhappy in a life which consisted merely of a fleeting, vanishing present and is now over and finished.[76]

In other words, since everyone, in the end, "reaches the port" with broken masts and ripped sails, it makes no difference whether one person was "successful" and another not. Because the name of this "port", for all of us equally, is death:

And so the course of a man's life is, as a rule, that, having been duped by hope, he dances into the arms of death.[77]

In summary, then: the blind will-to-live causes us to suffer in six distinct ways. Firstly, we are constantly desperately pursuing the satisfaction of our needs; secondly, these needs recur endlessly just the same; thirdly, we are also constantly preoccupied by the question of future needs; fourthly, the individualized will involves us inevitably in a "war of all against all"; fifthly, our lives are an endless pendulum swing between anxious care and boredom; and sixthly, death overshadows all that the will-to-live creates and sustains.

The Blind Will-to-Live in History

Just as the blind will-to-live manifests itself in each individual, so too does it manifest itself in the huge collective movements that make up world history:

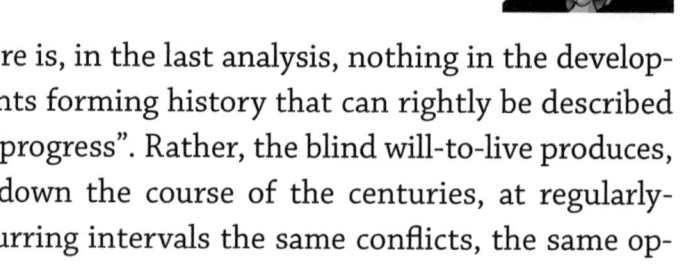

If we attempt to take in at a glance the whole world of humanity, we see everywhere a restless struggle, a vast contest for life and existence, with the fullest exertion of bodily and mental powers [...].[78]

There is, in the last analysis, nothing in the developments forming history that can rightly be described as "progress". Rather, the blind will-to-live produces, all down the course of the centuries, at regularly-recurring intervals the same conflicts, the same oppressions and the same revolts against oppression:

History shows us the life of nations and can find nothing to relate except wars and insurrections; the years of peace appear here and there only as short pauses, as intervals between the acts.[79]

This fact that peace between human beings is the exception rather than the rule and arises, as Schopenhauer points out, only "here and there" for brief intervals must necessarily prompt the question: "Why is this so? Are human beings not able to draw conclusions from all the suffering that they heap upon themselves, driven on by the will-to-live?" Schopenhauer does pose this question but remains, here too, pessimistic. There have indeed, he says, always been individual wise men who have been able really to learn from history. But they have exerted little influence, or none at all:

In general, indeed, the wise in all ages have always said the same things and the fools, who always form the immense majority, have in their way too acted alike, and done just the opposite. And so it will continue [...].[80]

And since the "immense majority", since time immemorial, have always done the very opposite to what the wise recommended, there can be no real progress. The egoism of human beings, and their constant fighting with one another, will always prevent that. Not even the state, which has been praised by so many political theorists as an agent of progress inasmuch as it causes individuals to cease to use violence on one another and to co-exist in peace, is, for Schopenhauer, no real guarantee of harmony:

[...] The dissension and discord of individuals can never be wholly eliminated by the state for they irritate and annoy in trifles where they are prohibited in great things.[81]

The constant strife and struggle that has accompanied human existence from the very beginning finds its mythological expression in the Ancient Greek goddess Eris, known indeed as "the Goddess of Strife and Discord". Eris, argues Schopenhauer, is as "immortal" as mythology makes her out to be; she can never be permanently driven away by any law or rule, however rational:

> As the conflict of individuals (Eris) is banished by the institution of the state; but she enters again, from without, as war between nations and demands in bulk and all at once [...] the bloody sacrifices that had been withheld from her by wise precaution.[82]

But even if Mankind were somehow to succeed at last, unexpectedly, in the course of the next few hundred years, in learning from history and putting an end to wars, not even this, argues Schopenhauer, would provide a way out of suffering:

> Even supposing all this were finally overcome and removed by prudence based on the experience of thousands of years, the result in the end would be the [...]

over-population of the whole planet, the terrible evil of which only a bold imagination can conjure up in the mind.[83]

This warning about the "terrible evil" of over-population is not just yet one more indication of the philosopher's deep pessimism but, besides this, also one of how astonishingly prescient his analyses of the power of the "blind will-to-live" were. This threat to the life of the whole planet which he envisages in the form of over-population has today taken concrete form as global famines, great waves of migration prompted by these famines, destruction of the environment, wars for raw materials, for territory and for water supplies and other terrible events. Particularly worthy of meditation, perhaps, is Schopenhauer's early observation that, in human history, "the majority have always done the opposite to what the few wise men recommended".

Thus, for example, the Club of Rome warned as early as 1972, with its famous report on *The Limits to Growth*, that continued population growth, and the continued growth of economic activity itself, would likely lead to a general collapse of the world eco-system, and demanded, therefore, some sort of sustainable programme of global population control. But precisely the opposite course has been taken, in the last fifty years, to that recommended by these scientists. Since 1972, world population has grown from 3.8 billion to 7.3 billion and will, according to projections by the UN, most likely pass the 10 billion mark by 2050. As Schopenhauer argued, the sexual urge is such a profound and powerful objectification of the blind will-to-live that it is unlikely that any government will be able, even in future, to set effective limits to it.

Schopenhauer's great philosophical rival, Hegel, by contrast, is famous for having portrayed human history in the very contrary terms to these: as a constant progress and development to higher and higher stages of the lives of nations and cultures, driven on and suffused by reason and moral spirit. But if this were really so, Schopenhauer retorted to his rival, there would surely be some palpable proof of it:

> The oft-repeated doctrine of a progressive development of Mankind to an ever higher perfection [...] is opposed to the *a priori* view that, up to any
>
> given point in time, an infinite time has already passed and, consequently, all that is supposed to come with time is bound to have existed already.[84]

According to Schopenhauer, we can observe no real progress in either a political, a moral, or an ethical sense across the whole vast expanse of time between the barbaric beginnings of human civilization, with all their archaic rituals, and the present day. One might argue, for example, that the forms of politeness and etiquette are signs that we have become a more "highly developed" humanity. But Schopenhauer sees no essential difference between the most primitive jungle dances and the formalized solemnities seen at the royal courts of the most exquisitely civilized nations:

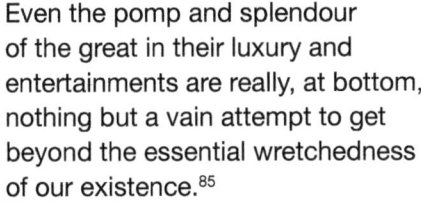

Even the pomp and splendour of the great in their luxury and entertainments are really, at bottom, nothing but a vain attempt to get beyond the essential wretchedness of our existence.[85]

But even "the great", in the end, stand no better chance of "getting beyond the essential wretchedness of our existence" than do the "little people". Nor does the future promise any improvement here:

The true philosophy of history thus consists in the insight that, in spite of all these endless changes and their chaos and confusion, we yet

always have before us only the same identical, unchangeable essence, acting in the same way today as it did yesterday and always [...].[86]

The genuine symbol of Nature is universally and everywhere the circle [...].[87]

We simply turn, then, always in a circle. Our rational understanding is incapable of improving, or of influencing in any way, the history of the objectification of the blind will-to-live. Nations, cultures and human beings arise, exist for a time, and are then submerged once again. And from their ashes there emerge new nations, cultures and individuals:

Every individual [...] and (his) course of life is only one more short dream of the endless spirit of Nature, of the persistent will-to-live [...] (which) is allowed to exist for a short while and is then effaced, to make new room.[88]

The Blind Will-to-Live and God

But why does the blind will do this? Why does it take the trouble to manifest itself in the form of Man, as well as of all the other organisms, if all this is, in the end, without sense or purpose? And above all: why does the will mount, across the whole planet, this great spectacle of cannibalistic eating and being eaten in which plants, animals and human beings all take part? Schopenhauer himself asked himself this question:

What is the point of this whole scene of horror? The only answer is that the will-to-live thus objectifies itself.[89]

No more, it appears, is possible than just this blunt registration of the fact that it is so, and not otherwise, that the will takes material form. Human beings, however, Schopenhauer points out, have great difficulty accepting this simple truth. They have always sought after some more beautiful explanation:

Man creates for himself in his own image demons, gods and saints; then to these must be incessantly offered sacrifices, prayers [...] vows and their fulfilment.[90]

Every human being, argues Schopenhauer, feels a need for some sort of comprehensive explanation of the meaning of the world:

Temples and churches, pagodas and mosques, in all countries and all ages [...] testify to Man's need for metaphysics [...].[91]

It is no wonder, then, that religious explanations for the meaning of life and death began to emerge already with the first emergence of consciousness. Both the Bible and the Koran give, in the last analysis, the same comforting answer: Man does not have to die but rather lives on, provided only that he believes and keeps the faith, in the world beyond. All these religions preach basically the same thing: that an all-powerful, loving God created the world in order to test human beings and, if they passed this test, reward them with eternal life. But such explanations, Schopenhauer points out, have foundered, from the very beginning, on what is called the "theodicy" problem. They cannot explain why a Creator God who is, at the same time, loving and all-powerful would possibly have created also such things as fatal illnesses and terrible natural catastrophes. The issue in need of explanation here is called "the theodicy problem" because this latter term is a composite of the ancient Greek words *theos*, meaning "god", and *dike*, meaning "justice" or "justification". The problem is that of "justifying" God in the face of all the evil in the world that we must, if God is all-powerful, take to have been created or at least permitted by Him.

The last great attempt at such a "justifying of God" was undertaken by the German philosopher Leibniz in his well-known theory of "the best of all possible worlds". God, argued Leibniz, had indeed built into the world He created such bad things as sickness, death, pain and even the possibility of moral failure; nevertheless, this was still the best of all the possible worlds He could have created. Because, were it not for sickness, Man would not appreciate health; were it not for war, he would not appreciate peace; and were it not for evil, he would not appreciate the good. Schopenhauer calls Leibniz, as the inventor of this theory, "the founder of systematic optimism"[92] and rejects, naturally, Leibniz's whole perspective here. In the face of the reality we actually live in, says Schopenhauer, to speak of "the best of all possible worlds" and of "a masterpiece of God's creation" is the most glaring absurdity:

This world is the battleground of tormented and agonized beings who continue to exist only by each devouring the other. Therefore, each beast of prey in it is the living grave

of thousands of others [...] In this world, the capacity to feel pain increases with knowledge and therefore reaches the highest degree

in Man [...] To this world the attempt has been made to adapt the system of optimism and to demonstrate to us that it is the best of all possible worlds. The absurdity is glaring.[93]

Schopenhauer inverts Leibniz's famous thesis and directs it back at him. Our world, he argues, is not the best of all possible worlds but, on the contrary, the worst of all possible ones:

This world is arranged as it had to be if it were to be capable of continuing, with great difficulty, to exist. If it were a little worse, it would no longer be capable of continuing to exist.[94]

The world, in other words, is so bad that, if it were even a tiny bit worse, it would be impossible for us to bear it and to continue to exist in it. Needless to say, Schopenhauer was a convinced atheist. He absolutely rejected the religious notion whereby all suffering in the world is either a punishment of Man by God or some form of God's "testing" of the chosen creature "created in His image". If this were so, Schopenhauer asked, why do dumb animals appear to have to suffer the same terrible punishments?

All "theodicy" then, Schopenhauer concludes, ultimately founders on the fact of its inability to explain the terrible suffering that exists in the world. Because a God conceived of as both loving and all-powerful cannot also be conceived of as the agent causing all this suffering. If God has indeed created all this suffering, then God must also take on and bear the responsibility for it. Of all the various religious Creation myths, then, it is the Creation myth of Hinduism that Schopenhauer finds most sensible and appealing:

Brahma produces the world through a kind of original sin, but himself remains in it to atone for this until he has redeemed himself from it. This is quite a good idea![95]

The Judaeo-Christian Creation myth of the Old Testament, by contrast, seems to Schopenhauer "intolerable":

That a God should create this world of misery and affliction [...] and then applaud himself with a "...and He found that it was very good", this is something intolerable.[96]

Finally, Schopenhauer also rejects all religious Creation myths by reason of their being mere speculation. The descriptions we find in them of Heaven and of Hell look to him to be extremely "man-made". This even applies to perhaps the most famous and most brilliant description of Hell, the first book, entitled *Inferno*, of Dante's *Divine Comedy*, composed in the first twenty years of the 14th century. Dante here, argues Schopenhauer, certainly based his work more on human than divine models:

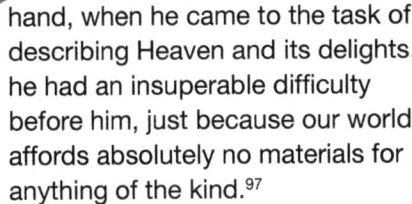

From whence did Dante get the material for his Hell, if not from this actual world of ours? And indeed he made a downright Hell of it. On the other hand, when he came to the task of describing Heaven and its delights, he had an insuperable difficulty before him, just because our world affords absolutely no materials for anything of the kind.[97]

It is, indeed, a frequently expressed testimony of readers who get so far into Dante's great work as the culminating *Paradise* that this long description of Heaven makes, particularly when set next to the striking scenes of Dante's Hell, a rather pale and insubstantial impression, having little more to draw on than a few revered descriptions by ancient Church Fathers. Already as a very young man, Schopenhauer had noted down in his *Travel Diaries*:

If a God created this world, I would not want to be that God; its misery would tear my heart in two.[98]

As a convinced atheist, Schopenhauer naturally also asked himself the question: if there is no God, then what exactly does the meaning of life consist in? His answer is clear enough:

[...] No one has the remotest idea why the whole tragi-comedy exists, for it has no spectators and the actors themselves undergo endless worry and trouble with [...] little enjoyment.[99]

Only partially are certain suffering human beings "spectators" to the worry and trouble of certain others:

The doctor sees Man in all his weakness; the lawyer sees him in all his wickedness; and the theologian sees him in all his folly and stupidity.[100]

Neither God nor the Devil, nor any other sort of extra-worldly being, are looking down on us, nor did they stage this weakness, wickedness and folly for any reason at all. We, the actors, must play our wretched roles our whole lives long. But we owe no one our "thanks" for this, least of all any Creator God such as is preached to us by priests and theologians from their pulpits.

We should not allow ourselves, then, to be made stupid by religion. To live means to suffer. We can neither find comfort in the face of this fact from the thought of a loving Creator, nor can we shift the blame for it onto the Devil or some other evil spirit. Just why the metaphysical will-to-live has objectified itself in the form of us and our world we do not know. We only know that it has done so:

[…] The only answer is that the will-to-live thus objectifies itself.[101]

But if we muster the courage to acknowledge this and to see the world and our own nature for what they really are, namely "blind will" without any transcendent sense or meaning to it, then we will surely be in a position better to handle the challenges of life.

Compassion as the Basis of Ethics

Like all great philosophers, Schopenhauer too composed an "ethics", that is to say, a doctrine of what it is to act well and rightly. Initially, it may seem impossible, given what we have already said about Schopenhauer's thought, that he should have set about doing such a thing. How, we might ask, would human beings even be capable of doing what is right and good if we are constantly driven on, in all our actions, by a blind and hungry "will-to-live"? Does Schopenhauer himself not lengthily portray egoism as the basic, essential attitude of human beings toward the world and relations between these human beings, consequently, as a constant struggle of all against all?

The fact is that Schopenhauer never moves from this position. He nevertheless is able to point up a possible way in which, at least on occasion, human beings might prove to be capable of non-selfish action. Schopenhauer deduces this possibility, highly logically consistently, from the premisses of his metaphysics of the will. Human beings will tend to act selflessly and in a morally good way where they come to recognize the blind universal will that is driving them onward to be something that is operative also in other living beings. The person who recognizes this will begin to become aware that these other human beings, just like himself, are helplessly driven creatures who all suffer from their inability to fulfil their wishes and their needs. With this awareness there intuitively arises also a sense of pity or compassion. In the best of cases, such a person may even succeed in empathizing totally and absolutely with the suffering of another human being:

> [...] The suffering he sees in others touches him almost as closely as does his own. He therefore tries to strike a balance between the two, denies himself pleasures, undergoes privations, in order to alleviate another's suffering.[102]

Morally good action, then, arises, according to Schopenhauer, out of the wish "to alleviate another's suffering". Since, however, our essential nature continues to dictate that we remain egoistic beings interested above all in our own survival and our own welfare, the maxim governing and guiding our actions needs to be the following:

> Do good to yourself with as little evil as possible to others.[103]

This even applies, Schopenhauer argues, to animals:

Compassion for animals goes together with goodness of character so precisely that we can confidently assert that anyone who is cruel to animals cannot be a good human being.[104]

By helping other living beings and putting aside our own egoistic needs and wishes, we act morally. But this phenomenon of pity, Schopenhauer takes great care to stress, is not something which results from a good Christian or humanistic upbringing or from the careful observance of some such moral maxim as Kant's "categorical imperative". It is, at bottom, simply and solely a matter of the true perception of our own inner nature:

This compassion [...] does not rest on presuppositions, concepts, religions, dogmas, myths, upbringing and education but [...] resides in human nature itself.[105]

If we come directly face to face with the suffering of our neighbour there will tend to announce itself our own natural urge of self-preservation, i.e. our will-to-live, giving us to understand that this same will feels threatened in the objectified form that it has taken in our neighbour. That is to say, a human being recognizes, in this moment, his own will-to-live in the other person:

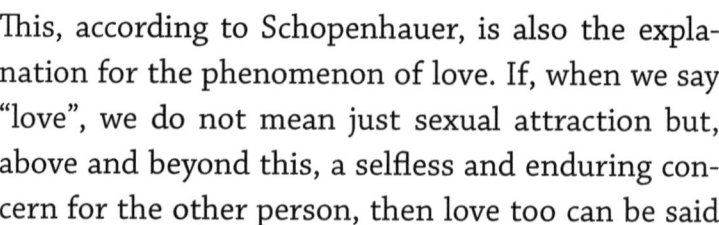

He perceives that the distinction between himself and others [...] belongs only to a fleeting, deceptive phenomenon. He recognizes immediately, and

without reasons and arguments, that the in-itself of his own phenomenon is also that of others, namely that will-to-live which constitutes the inner nature of everything.[106]

This, according to Schopenhauer, is also the explanation for the phenomenon of love. If, when we say "love", we do not mean just sexual attraction but, above and beyond this, a selfless and enduring concern for the other person, then love too can be said to be a form of pity, an empathetic recognition of oneself in the other:

From this it follows that pure love [...] is, by its nature, sympathy.[107]

This empathy with the fate of others really succeeds indeed, Schopenhauer admits, only very rarely in our daily lives. Mostly, the will-to-live ensures that people's attitude toward others will not be compassionate but rather egoistic. For this reason, the average human being is inclined rather to hide his pain from others

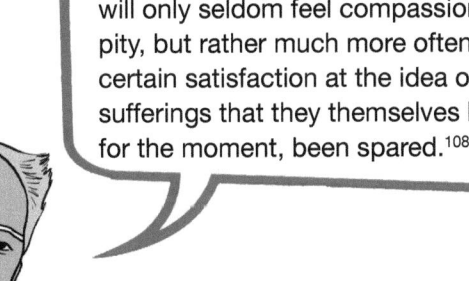

[...] because he knows that others will only seldom feel compassion or pity, but rather much more often a certain satisfaction at the idea of the sufferings that they themselves have, for the moment, been spared.[108]

The sight of others' suffering can often make a person's own woes appear less grave and help him to deal with them. For this reason, a certain satisfaction at others' pain frequently crowds out the impulse of pity, so that, in the end, human beings remain the egotistic beings in constant competition with one another that the will-to-live makes us:

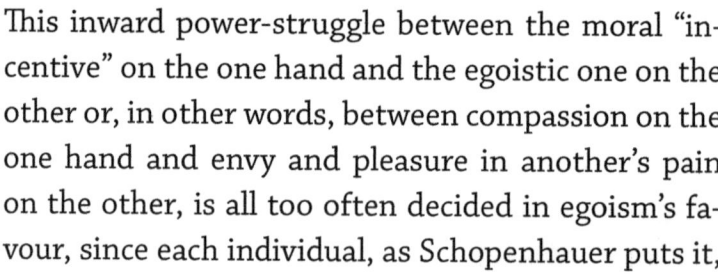

The chief and fundamental incentive in a human being, as in an animal, is egoism, i.e. the urge to existence and wellbeing [...] This egoism, both in an animal and in a human being, is linked in the most precise way with his innermost core and essence, and indeed is properly identical with it. [...] Egoism, then, is the first and principal power [...] that the moral incentive has to combat.[109]

This inward power-struggle between the moral "incentive" on the one hand and the egoistic one on the other or, in other words, between compassion on the one hand and envy and pleasure in another's pain on the other, is all too often decided in egoism's favour, since each individual, as Schopenhauer puts it, "is given to himself immediately", while others are "given to him only mediately, by way of the representation of them in his head."[110]

The Triple Overcoming of the Will in Art, Theatre and Ascetic Practice

Schopenhauer sums up the result of his considerations regarding the will in a single sentence:

Therefore, so long as our consciousness is filled by our will, so long as we are given up to the throng of desires with its constant hopes and fears, so long as we are the subject of willing, we never attain lasting happiness or peace.[111]

There are only three possible ways out of this restless state of being driven back and forth by our willing. The first of these is the making, and the enjoyment, of art. When we contemplate a work of art and allow it to exert its effect upon us, our life ceases for a moment to be that selfishly goal-directed thing it otherwise is:

(This is the state of) pure contemplation, absorption in perception, being lost in the object, forgetting all individuality [...].[112]

Following Kant, Schopenhauer looked on art as essentially a "disinterested pleasure". That is to say, for the few moments that we spend absorbed in genuine contemplation or enjoyment of a work of art, we are no longer guided and governed by the blind will-to-live. Because this blind will-to-live has, at all times, one or another specific goal or aim that it is pursuing. When we are hungry, we aim to acquire food; when we are erotically aroused, we seek sexual congress. The effect exerted upon us by a work of art, however, is of a quite different nature. We can neither eat the work of art nor render it useful for the purposes of some other among our drives or urges. A purely aesthetic pleasure has a different, an entirely new, dimension:

For that moment we are delivered from the miserable pressure of the will. We celebrate the Sabbath of the penal servitude of willing. The wheel of Ixion stands still.[113]

This "wheel of Ixion", which Schopenhauer speaks of as "standing still" in the moment in which we contemplate a work of art, was an instrument of torture described in one of the myths of the ancient Greeks. King Ixion attempted, when drunk, to seduce Hera, the wife of Zeus, king of all the gods and was punished by being bound, for all eternity, to a constantly revolving ring of fire. Schopenhauer uses the image of a man's feelings on being finally unbound, even if only for a moment, from such an instrument of torture to express the notion of the contemplation of the work of art's freeing us from the constant sway of the blind will. He also calls such a moment the "sabbath" of our subjection to this will, i.e. the brief "day of rest" in which we are relieved of the "hard labour" that is our endless, driven pursuit of goals. In contemplating the work of art, be this a timelessly beautiful picture or a perfect statue, we are able finally to forget our ego and leave it behind us. The artists themselves, indeed, do not represent in their works just what their blind will drives them to desire but rather seek also to bring to expression that timeless idea of the Good and the Beautiful which lies behind all phenomena. That is to say, a painter, for example, does not, in his paintings, simply show beautiful men or women in beautiful landscapes but rather attempts to seize and express the Idea of the Beautiful itself:

> The gift of genius is nothing but the most complete objectivity [...] In other words, the ability to leave entirely out of sight our own interest, our willing [...] in order to remain pure knowing subject, the clear eye of the world [...].[114]

This effect is produced even more intensely by music. When we hear a particularly moving composition, it can often happen that we become completely lost in the music. In contrast to the graphic and plastic arts, however, which direct our attention away from our day-to-day willing and toward the timeless Ideas, the art of music actually stresses and foregrounds the omnipresence of the will:

Therefore, music is by no means like the other arts, namely a copy of the Ideas, but *a copy of the Will itself*.[115]

In music, the will-to-live is actually directly reflected in every one of its aspects and elements, one by one. The lower, deeper tones stand here for the operation of this will in matter, in the form of gravity. The middle and higher tones, on the other hand, stand for animate Nature: the world of human beings and other animals. The dramatic shifts from one musical register into another, the rise and fall of rhythm and melody, give embodiment to the sorrows, joys, victories and defeats of life:

For this reason the effect of music is so very much more powerful and penetrating than is that of the other arts [...].[116]

When enjoying music and the other arts we become dissolved into the universal Will and are thus distracted from our willing in its individualized, personal form.

The second way out of our everyday state of being constantly driven hither and thither by the Will is the visiting of theatrical performances or the immersing of ourselves in correspondingly dramatic forms of literature:

[...] Every work of fiction is a peep-show in which we observe the spasms and convulsions of the agonized human heart.[117]

Such an experience, however, can only be really moving if we are able really to identify with the hero or heroine of the fiction and with his or her fears and anxieties. For this reason, playwrights must model their protagonists on real people like ourselves and must have them suffer, in the fictional world, much in the way that the spectators or readers of the fiction suffer in the real one. Indeed, it is expedient that they should suffer even more:

Therefore, all poets are obliged to bring their heroes into anxious and painful situations in order to be able to liberate them therefrom again. Accordingly, dramas and epics generally describe only fighting, tormented, suffering men and women [...].[118]

First, the poet artfully lists the different forms and stages of suffering his protagonist has to undergo: how he strains and struggles, how he seems about to be broken on the wheel of the world. His enemies seem invincible and the woman of his dreams beyond his reach. But when, at the end of the novel or the play, the hero, to our great delight, overcomes all these enemies and can finally clasp in his arms the long-sought loved one, object of all his desires, the playwright is forced to employ a peculiar artistic trick:

(He) conducts (his) heroes to their goal through a thousand difficulties and dangers; and as soon as the goal is reached (he) quickly lets the curtain fall.[119]

The curtain is lowered on the play, or the final chapter closed in the novel, because the hero, from this point on, gets to live with the woman of his dreams, to share her daily life and to watch how she brushes her teeth every morning. Her ineffable charm, the mystery of her unattainability, thus begins to fade under the weight of daily routine. Even more importantly, he has defeated all his enemies. No one any longer either fears him or seeks to take his life. Indeed, no one any longer really pays him much notice. One day is now much like the next. And instead of his enemies the threat now waiting around every corner is of a quite different sort. It is boredom:

> Life presents itself initially as a task, namely that of gaining a livelihood [...] When this problem is solved [...]

> there comes the second problem of how to dispose of what we have got in order to ward off boredom. Like a bird of prey on the watch, this evil pounces on every life that has been made secure.[120]

It is precisely for this reason that the curtain must fall so quickly. The spectator must not be robbed of the illusion of happiness. And indeed nobody wants to learn how Romeo and Juliet, after a few years' marriage, decide to divorce and go their separate ways due to a quarrel over a badly cooked egg. Nor does anyone want to watch James Bond growing old in dressing gown and slippers, sipping his martinis in front of the fire:

Every epic or dramatic poem can always present to us only a strife, an effort, and a struggle for happiness, never enduring and complete happiness itself.[121]

By showing us a skilfully chosen portion of reality, playwrights can fascinate us and distract us from our own conditions as creatures driven hither and thither by the will. We recognize, indeed, our own suffering in the suffering of the piece's protagonist; but at the same time we can maintain an objectifying distance from this suffering, since we do not have to "will" and "act" in the piece ourselves but rather see everything, as Schopenhauer puts it, as if through the slot of a "peep-show".

It remains, however, decidedly the case, as Schopenhauer insists on reminding us, that the experience of the graphic and plastic arts, music and theatre can serve, at best, to release us from the personal grip that the will-to-live has on each of us for just a few minutes or hours at a time. No more lasting liberation is possible except where we say "no" in basic principle to life and to all life's pleasures as well as to its sufferings:

Because the less the Will is stimulated, the less suffering there is [...].[122]

But "saying 'no' to life" does not mean, for Schopenhauer, that we should commit suicide. On the contrary, the person who commits suicide fails, precisely, to solve the essential problem, since his action of self-destruction does nothing to affect or alter the essential fact of the Will:

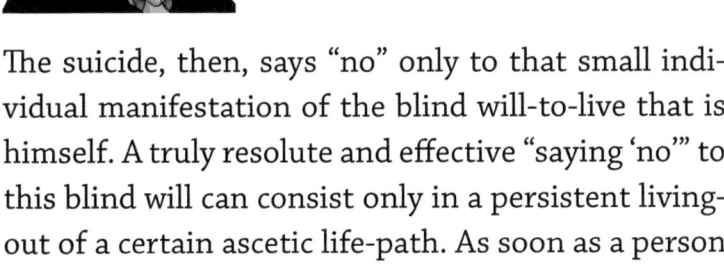

Far from being denial of the Will [...] (the man who commits suicide) by no means gives up the will-to-live [...] since he destroys (only) the individual phenomenon [...] The suicide denies merely the individual, not the species.[123]

The suicide, then, says "no" only to that small individual manifestation of the blind will-to-live that is himself. A truly resolute and effective "saying 'no'" to this blind will can consist only in a persistent living-out of a certain ascetic life-path. As soon as a person resolves to deny life in itself

[...] He ceases to will anything, guards against attaching his will to anything [...] Voluntary and complete chastity is the first step in asceticism

[...] Asceticism then also expresses itself in the form of voluntary and deliberate poverty.[124]

Just as Buddhism has taught for many centuries already, the way for Man is not to let himself be distracted by external things but rather to concentrate, through asceticism and meditation, on that profound experience of all-in-oneness which brings it about that he

> [...] no longer makes the egoistical distinction between himself and the person of others [...] so that it follows automatically that such a man (recognizes) in all beings his own true and innermost self [...].[125]

But this experience of recognizing one's own true being in all other living things means nothing less, Schopenhauer emphatically points out, than the dissolution of the individual self and a passing over into a state of "nirvana", or nothingness:

> [...] We freely acknowledge that what remains after the complete abolition of the will is, for all those who are still full

of the will, assuredly nothing. But also, conversely, to those in whom the will has turned and denied itself, this very real world of ours with all its suns and galaxies is – nothing.[126]

This "nirvana experience" of feeling and knowing the real world, with all its suns and planets, to be "nothing", in the sense that we become a part of it and are dissolved into it, was, Schopenhauer points out, quite rightly described by the Buddhists and the sages who authored the Indian Upanishads as the highest stage of enlightenment. In contrast to the mass of ordinary human beings, the enlightened person has recognized that the egoism that had characterized his life up to the point of his enlightenment had arisen only due to the natural principle of the blind will's "individuation" of itself into competing singular individuals. He has now, however, "seen through" this appearance of his own blind will as something singular and recognized it to be part of a universal world-will, thus raising himself above this will's hungry restlessness:

> [...] Seeing through the *principium individuationis*, everything lies equally near to him. He knows the whole, comprehends its inner nature, and finds it involved in a constant passing away, a vain striving [...].[127]

But a human being who rises so far above the nugatory, egoistic striving of the individual wills acting and operating in the world, and who feels himself, to this degree, united with the universe as a whole, thereby also abolishes himself as subject and individual. To describe this experience Schopenhauer uses the famous Sanskrit phrase so central to Indian religions *tat tvam asi*, meaning "that art thou". In other words, the individual "I" is only an illusion we have been befooled by for many thousands of years. The only true reality is "the infinite Oneness". If one just observes and contemplates, lengthily and deeply enough, the plants and the animals in their free, natural state, one begins to recognize one's own self in them and to understand intuitively this profound Eastern wisdom:

Tat tvam asi, meaning "this living thing art thou".[128]

We can have this experience of "all-in-oneness" with other living beings because the universal will-to-live, even when it manifests itself in the form of millions of apparently distinct beings, is in the last analysis one and the same Will. Schopenhauer himself engaged in long, philosophically reflective examinations and observations of plants and animals, spending hours, for example in the Dresden Botanical Gardens:

The objective contemplation of the many different and marvellous forms (of plants and animals) [...] is an instructive lesson from the great book of Nature [...] We see in it [...] the manifestation of the Will [...] But if we

had to convey to the beholder [...] their inner nature, it would be best for us to use the Sanskrit formula which occurs so often in the sacred books of the Hindus and is called the *mahavakya*, the "great word": *tat tvam asi*, which means 'this living thing art thou'.[129]

Of What Use Is Schopenhauer's Discovery for Us Today?

Can We Escape the Blind Will Through Asceticism?

Schopenhauer was completely convinced that his key idea of a "blind" and "hungry" will, along with its "denial" through ascetic practice would still find an audience centuries after his formulating it. And he seems to have been right. There is now greater and greater interest in his philosophy all over the world. But of what use is his great discovery for us today? Can we really say "no" to life and escape the "blind will" through meditation and other ascetic practices? Is the "yoga boom" of recent years perhaps a first indication of people's attitudes to life and the world changing in a sense that Schopenhauer would have greeted? Or must such things as asceticism and withdrawal from the world through meditation remain, for people raised in and formed by the West, in the end just ways of fooling and deluding ourselves?

Schopenhauer was a realist and he remained rather

sceptical regarding the consequences likely to ensue from his philosophy of the "blind will-to-live". It was logical and understandable, he thought, that the "blind will" should be rejected. But he qualified his call for this "saying 'no' to life", this "dissolution into the World-Soul", this *tat tvam asi* and this attainment of Nirvana with a recognition that these were, really, only prospects that presented themselves where his philosophy was consistently theoretically developed. That is to say, he warned his readers against any great optimism regarding the prospects of actually practically achieving such things. It was an extremely difficult thing, he said, to "say 'no' to the blind will", since this latter has governed and led us all since our births. Only a very few great sages and holy men, such as the Buddha, have ever really achieved this. It is in the faces of such rare individuals alone that we see reflected

[...] That peace that is higher than all reason, that ocean-like calmness of the spirit, that deep tranquillity, that unshakeable confidence and serenity [...].[130]

These exceptional human beings have left their driving and driven ego behind, have become one with all that is, and have succeeded in genuinely realizing the Vedic formula:

Tat tvam asi! ("that art thou"). Whoever is able to declare this to himself with clear knowledge and

firm inward conviction about every creature with whom he comes into contact is certain of all virtue and bliss and is on the direct path to salvation.[131]

But such a step into "all-in-one-ness", into Nirvana, and thereby into a spiritual state of complete wish- and willless-ness, will always only be possible for a very small portion of humanity. Certainly, Schopenhauer himself never achieved such a state. He did not engage, to any great degree, in meditation nor did he live a very ascetic life. He was known, indeed, to be something of a gourmet. The French philosopher Camus, for example, reproaches him in one of his books with having "preached the refusal of life between the third and fourth course at a well-served table". Schopenhauer was aware of his own personal inconsistency here but argued that what mattered was not him or his personal behaviour but rather the truth of the philosophy he advanced:

It is just as little necessary for a philosopher to be a saint as it is for a great sculptor to be himself a beautiful person.[132]

Philosophy's task, Schopenhauer argues, is, in basic principle, a quite different one:

To repeat abstractly, universally, and distinctly, in concepts always ready for the faculty of reason, the whole inner nature of the world […] this and nothing else is philosophy.[133]

In the end, then, Schopenhauer contented himself, in the way of adopting an "ascetic style of life", with just buying a large Tibetan statue of the Buddha to decorate his apartment. He placed it, indeed, in a prominent position and was always pleased when visitors noticed and commented on it. He also sometimes went so far as to describe himself, and also those followers of his philosophy who became more numerous toward the end of his life, as "Buddhists". This, however, was just an expression of how close he stood, theoretically, to the Buddhist doctrine of "renunciation of the world" and how much he admired it. The same most likely applies to the much more numerous Western households boasting Buddhistic figures and motifs today. These figures sit at home emanating tranquillity and serenity while the owners of the homes in question struggle frantically to get ahead in the jungle-like capitalist metropolises outside the windows. Nevertheless, even if one cannot follow the path of pure asceticism, as indeed Schopenhauer himself could not, there emerges from Schopenhauer's philosophy another attitude to life in the world which is perhaps more within the reach of the average modern human being.

Schopenhauer arrived, in the first place, at the conclusion that higher life-forms suffer far more than do lower ones; secondly, he concluded that we intuitively sense that the same will-to-live is operative both in human beings and in animals; thirdly, he advanced the moral rule that we should act in such a way as to inflict as little suffering as possible on living beings. If one takes all of these three thoughts together, there emerges a maxim which is perhaps more feasibly to be observed by modern human beings than the ideal of total asceticism: namely, that of respecting the right of all living beings to life and bodily integrity:

(Therefore) in Europe too the sense of the rights of animals is awakening more and more [...].[134]

"Think Positive" as Ideological Deceit: Schopenhauer's Plea for Pessimism.

"Think positive!", "Live your best life!": today, we are all bombarded daily and even hourly by slogans and exhortations of this kind. Only someone who is himself highly motivated, we are told, can motivate others. Enthusiasm is the key to a brilliant career. It is hard to imagine a man like Schopenhauer getting by in today's society even as modestly well as he did in the society of the mid-19th century. Our "high-performance" world demands a high degree of optimism as the most basic of prerequisites, a sort of oil in the engine of capitalism. "Looking on the dark side" has, of course, never been a quality apt to make one welcome in company intent on moving forward and improving things. But in our late modern era "positive thinking" seems to be becoming almost compulsory. Optimism is treated as if it were a basic duty of every citizen. Anyone who displays a critical disposition, an air of discomfort or, God forbid, gives the impression of being depressed is immediately surrounded by people urging, or even forcing on him "self-help" literature or various forms of coaching, personal training or psychotherapy.

Schopenhauer is surely turning in his grave. This constant chorus of "positive thinking" and "being the best one can be" would seem to him to be an enormous ideology of self-deceit. It certainly is just that when promulgated in the context of our globalized capitalist economy, because "being the best one can be" generally means being the most efficient worker for one's employer, not pursuing real fulfilment for oneself. But Schopenhauer, in fact, is opposed to optimism as a life-attitude in any context:

I cannot here withhold the statement that optimism [...] seems to me not merely an absurd but also a really *wicked* way of thinking, a bitter mockery of the unspeakable sufferings of mankind.[135]

Furthermore, there simply happen to be certain people whose character is such that they tend to look at the world and at themselves more critically than do most people. And for Schopenhauer this is certainly not a bad kind of character to have or any sort of "condition" that needs to be "cured" away but rather an authentic and insightful attitude. Especially gifted people do tend to suffer especially intensely from life in the world:

[...] The capacity to feel pain increases with knowledge and therefore reaches its highest degree in Man, a degree that is the higher the more intelligent the man.[136]

But pessimism is not only more authentic than optimism; it is also a greater practical help in life. It may appear to be a "dark and fearful" attitude to life but it tends nonetheless to prove the more successful one because:

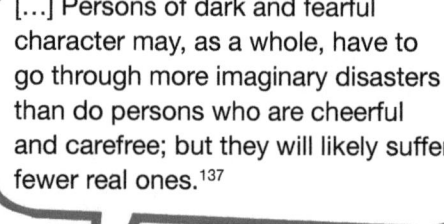

[...] Persons of dark and fearful character may, as a whole, have to go through more imaginary disasters than do persons who are cheerful and carefree; but they will likely suffer fewer real ones.[137]

The pessimist, since he always expects the worst, will tend to act correspondingly cautiously. The optimist, however, always expecting a positive outcome, will often not recognize the real risks.

Schopenhauer himself might be seen as a living illustration of this lesson. It was a well-known fact about him that he always took his own beer-glass with him when visiting a bar for fear of catching an infection. So when he heard, in 1831, that cholera had broken out in Berlin, where he had been living for some years, he immediately dropped all his business there and moved, first briefly to Mannheim, and then more permanently to Frankfurt, which city he felt, for some reason, to be infection-proof. His great philosophical rival at the University of Berlin, Hegel, by contrast, left the city only very briefly and on his early return became infected and died, at the relatively early age of sixty-one. We cannot be certain whether to put this down to Schopenhauer's personal cautiousness or to some deeper irony of Fate. It remains a fact, however, that Hegel, the great optimist who taught that the "real is the rational" and saw the World-Spirit walking in the earth, met his death, while the pessimist Schopenhauer survived.

Whoever Does Not Know His Age Will Surely Know That Age's Sufferings – Growing Old Realistically With Schopenhauer

The person feeling despondent at approaching old or even just middle age may sometimes hear the cheering words: "You're only as old as you feel". Ageing, they are told, is less a biological process than a state of mind. What's more, we are today surrounded by "anti-ageing" products that promise to halt even the biological process. Countless fitness programmes offer eternal conformity to the social ideal of youthful beauty. But Schopenhauer has another proposal. He recommends that we deal more realistically with the various succeeding stages of our lives. Citing his much-admired Voltaire, he writes:

Qui n'a pas l'esprit de son âge, de son âge a tout le malheur (whoever does not know his age will surely know that age's sufferings).[138]

That is to say, one must be careful, as one ages, to preserve a correct sense of one's powers and limitations and not, for example, to strain oneself physically in old age. Then perhaps, long walks, such as those which Schopenhauer himself took with his dog, are best for the health. A decline in physical and mental vigour is, indeed, inevitable but has its compensations. For example, the decline in the sexual urge in one's later years is, in some respects, an advantage:

It might even be asserted that the many different and endless whims and crotchets that are engendered by the sexual impulse and the emotions arising therefrom foster

in Man a perpetual mild madness. [...] so that he becomes rational only when the passion is extinguished.[139]

Whereas youth is passed entirely under "the sway of this demon" and suffers every sort of love-sickness and melancholy

> [...] old age has the cheerfulness of one who has rid himself of a shackle long borne and who now freely moves about.[140]

What is more, the pleasures of sexuality can be replaced, at this stage of life, by other sources of pleasure:

> Deserted by Venus, we gladly look for merriment and diversion in Bacchus.[141]

The place of the Goddess of Love is taken, then, by the God of Wine. Furthermore, Schopenhauer goes on, that older people tend to become bored offers a threefold advantage. When one is freed of the obligations of earning a living one finally gains free time in which one can put one's experiences to some use and attempt to understand life:

In all things, we attain an ever more comprehensive survey of the whole [...] so that our own real inner self-culture continues to make progress [...].[142]

Moreover, time passes much more rapidly in old age and this counteracts boredom.[143]

And thirdly, one is far more sparing with one's time in old age:

[...] In old age, one is careful how one spends one's time. One is like a man who, delving into his sack of money, finds he can already see the bottom.[144]

Schopenhauer concedes, however, that it is increasingly hard, as age advances, to find compensations for the dwindling of one's strength. *Getting Old Is Not For the Faint-Hearted* ran the title given to his memoirs by one famous German actor. This sums up Schopenhauer's own attitude to ageing. In the end, one must come to terms with the sufferings growing old brings, and indeed this coming to terms with them has a purpose and a benefit:

The disappearance of all our powers as we grow older is certainly very distressing. Yet this is necessary and even beneficial, because otherwise death would be too hard [...].[145]

Freeing Oneself from the Compulsion to Be Happy – Schopenhauer's Legacy

Schopenhauer's legacy is a many-layered one. The secondary literature usually mentions three important effects that his thought has had on posterity. Firstly, Schopenhauer's philosophy of a will that blindly and unconsciously guides our actions clearly inspired and prepared the way for the psychoanalysis of Sigmund Freud. Secondly, he quite rightly critiqued the exalted idea of Man as a being of pure spirit promoted by certain forms of philosophical idealism and thereby brought philosophy down to earth and factual reality once again. And thirdly, with his recommendations of ascetic practice, meditation and the pursuit of a spiritual path to "Nirvana" he was one of the first to open the West up to Buddhism and the philosophy of the Orient. His work, with its frequent references to Hindu and Buddhist texts, inspired a boom in translations of these ancient writings and certainly helped to prepare the ground for the wide use of yoga and meditation techniques in the western world today.

But his real legacy is to be sought in a much simpler context which is just for this reason often overlooked. Schopenhauer's philosophy can help us to free ourselves from what has become, today, a veritable compulsion to be happy and to "be the best we can be". Anyone who reads *The World as Will and Representation* will thenceforth be immune against this obsessive "be the best you can be" ideology of our modern societies. If one happens to be feeling bad, this is not necessarily a sign that one needs urgently to "do some work on oneself":

No man has ever yet felt entirely happy in the present, unless he were drunk.[146]

It can hardly be put more clearly than that. It lies, then, in the essential logic of Schopenhauer's philosophy that people have a fundamental right to be pessimistic, a right to be critical of human existence, even a right to "say 'no' to the whole world". This compulsion to be happy, indeed, is a phenomenon which has really only taken off in our own age, some while after Schopenhauer's. And in periods even earlier than his, of course, it was barely known at all. In the Middle Ages, suffering and unhappiness were looked on as sent by God to test us. Today, however, each person's unhappiness is looked on as their own fault and failing. The belief is that, if you are unhappy, you are clearly doing something wrong.

Those persuaded that they must seek to correct their error here find themselves faced with an enormous range of products claiming to be aids in their search to do so. On sale are self-improvement courses of a thousand different kinds, evoking oriental notions such as shamanism or Tantrism or simply inflating to extremes such Western notions as self-exploration with brand-names such as "Journey Into the Self". The book-market likewise offers more guides to "positive living" with each passing week. Just in the relatively small region of the world speaking Schopenhauer's native language, German, there were, at the last count, some 22,000 books on sale that featured the word "happiness" somewhere in their title. One can only imagine the bafflement and mild contempt with which Schopenhauer himself would have regarded all this:

We find a complete contradiction in our wishing to live without suffering.[147]

He would surely have responded to the promises contained in these "self-improvement" books, or to such other information characteristic of our present age as the news that the country of Bhutan has set up a Ministry for Happiness, with some bitterly ironic commentary. Already in 1818, in an age which had not yet moved nearly so far in this direction, we find him observing that it was a "strange error" to believe that "the inner disposition" could be altered by any measure taken by market or even by state:

As if the inner disposition [...], the eternally free will, could be modified from outside and changed by impression or influence![148]

And yet now, two hundred years later, every hair salon broadcasts, from its shop window, the promise that a half hour spent in their shop will "change who you are forever!" It is not only what is written down in his books that prompts one to believe that such publicity would be wasted on Schopenhauer, were he to be resurrected today. Schopenhauer was, indeed, always neatly dressed. But the hairstyle he affected was one that was, by the standards of his day, somewhat wild and eccentric, a feature noted in the famous drawing of the old philosopher by his friend Wilhelm Busch.

There can be no doubt but that Schopenhauer would have been no less of a nightmare client for the hairdresser than for the "life coach". He showed us in striking fashion that it is impossible in principle to remain absolutely happy for any length of time. Our will-to-live inundates us with more desires and wishes than reality can ever satisfy. And even if we succeed, for brief periods, in satisfying all our present desires, there remains the worry about desires and needs that may arise in the future:

> [...] So long as we are given up to the throng of desires, with its constant hopes and fears, so long as we are the subject of willing, we never obtain lasting happiness or peace.[149]

Schopenhauer says here what, in substance, the famous psychoanalyst Sigmund Freud was to say many years later: by his very constitution, Man is not made for happiness, since his imagination, or as Freud puts it his "fantasies", will always cause him to envisage more than reality can ever possibly fulfil. "One might say that Man's happiness is not part of the Creator's plan".[150] If Schopenhauer and Freud are right, then the happiness that is preached everywhere today is an illusion:

> A happy life is impossible; the best that man can attain is a heroic life [...].[151]

By living a "heroic life" Schopenhauer means persevering resolutely in our existence even while being driven to and fro by the will-to-live and suffering all the disappointments that this must necessarily bring. Our life also becomes a "heroic" one where we succeed in recognizing that the blind will-to-live that governs our own existence is also operative in all other living beings and in treating these living beings, for this reason, with forbearance:

> In fact, the conviction that the world, and thus also Man, is something that really ought not to be is calculated to fill us with forbearance toward one another.[152]

Since none of the inhabitants of this earth ever asked to be born, we all share the same fate. Schopenhauer proposes, therefore, that, instead of addressing one another with such traditional titles as "sir", "Herr", or "monsieur", there should be used henceforth, worldwide, only that one "really proper form or address between one man and another":

> [...] *socii malorum*, companion in misery, my fellow sufferer.[153]

Whoever succeeds, then, in fully grasping and taking to heart the spirit of Schopenhauer's philosophy will likely no longer be the plaything of our present-day "happiness industry". Such a person will know that death is inescapable and that the painful needs implanted in him by the blind will-to-live will accompany him all his life. But he will also know that he shares with all living beings one and the same wish for a whole and undamaged life. In short, he will live in full awareness of the contradictions of his own existence and will empathize with the pain of others while pursuing his own self-development, answering neither to God nor the Devil, as a soberly-thinking, critical mind and spirit. Schopenhauer himself pushed on resolutely down this path his entire life:

I suppose I shall have to be told again that my philosophy is cheerless and comfortless simply because I tell the truth [...].[154]

Bibliographical References

1   Arthur Schopenhauer, The World as Will and Representation,
    Dover Publications, New York, 1969 (two-volume edition), p. 581 of
    Volume Two.
2   Ibid. p. 360 of Volume Two.
3   Arthur Schopenhauer, Parerga and Paralipomena, Short Philosophical
    Essays, Volume 2, Oxford University Press, 1974, p. 601 of Volume
    Two.
4   Arthur Schopenhauer, The World as Will and Representation, Dover
    Publications, New York, 1969 (two-volume edition), p. 350 of Volume
    Two.
5   Ibid.
6   Ibid.
7   Ibid.
8   Ibid. p. 359 of Volume Two.
9   Ibid. p. 357 of Volume Two.
10 Ibid.
11 Ibid. p. 320 of Volume One.
12 Ibid. p. 350 of Volume One.
13 Ibid. p. 354 of Volume One.
14 Ibid.
15 Ibid. p. 466 of Volume Two.
16 Ibid. p. 351 of Volume Two.
17 Ibid. p. 89 of Volume Two.
18 Ibid. p. 349 of Volume Two.
19 Arthur Schopenhauer, Parerga and Paralipomena, Short Philosophical
    Essays, Volume 2, Oxford University Press, 1974, p. 300.
20 Ibid. p. 288.
21 Ibid. p. 299.
22 Arthur Schopenhauer, The World as Will and Representation, Dover
    Publications, New York, 1969 (two-volume edition), p. 576 of Volume
    Two.
23 Arthur Schopenhauer, Parerga and Paralipomena, Short Philosophical

Essays, Volume 2, Oxford University Press, 1974, p. 483.

24 " Atma" signifies "breath of life", or the individual soul conceived as part of Brahman, but it can also signify the "World-Soul" itself.

25 See Karl-Heinz Muscheler, Die Schopenhauer-Marquet Prozesse, Mohr-Siebeck Publishers, Tuebingen, 1996, p. 103.

26 Schopenhauer, Manuscript Remains, Volume 4, p. 119, cited in David E. Cartwright, Schopenhauer : A Biography, Cambridge University Press, 2010, p. 78.

27 Schopenhauer, Gespraeche, cited in David E. Cartwright, Schopenhauer : A Biography, Cambridge University Press, 2010, p. 149.

28 Schopenhauer, Reisetagebuecher, April 1804, cited in David E. Cartwright, Schopenhauer : A Biography, Cambridge University Press, 2010, p. 76.

29 Johanna Schopenhauer to her son, 6th November 1807, cited in David E. Cartwright, Schopenhauer : A Biography, Cambridge University Press, 2010, pp 129-130.

30 Arthur Schopenhauer, The World as Will and Representation, Dover Publications, New York, 1969 (two-volume edition), p. 325 of Volume Two.

31 Ibid. pp 379-380 of Volume Two.

32 Ibid. p. 3 of Volume One.

33 Ibid. p. 5 of Volume Two.

34 Arthur Schopenhauer, Prize Essay on the Basis of Morals, in The Two Fundamental Problems of Ethics, Cambridge Edition of the Works of Schopenhauer, Cambridge University Press, 2009, p. 191.

35 Arthur Schopenhauer, Parerga and Paralipomena, Short Philosophical Essays, Volume 1, Oxford University Press, 2015, p. 324.

36 Arthur Schopenhauer, The World as Will and Representation, Dover Publications, New York, 1969 (two-volume edition), p. 179 of Volume One.

37 Ibid. p. 100 of Volume One.

38 Ibid. p. 162 of Volume One.

39 Ibid. p. 109 of Volume One.

40 Arthur Schopenhauer, Handschriftlicher Nachlass, ed. by Arthur Huebscher, Munich, 1985, Vol 1, p. 462

41 Arthur Schopenhauer, The World as Will and Representation, Dover Publications, New York, 1969 (two-volume edition), p. 110 of Volume One.

42   Ibid. p. 350 of Volume Two.
43   Ibid. p. 358 of Volume Two.
44   Ibid. p. 287 of Volume One.
45   Ibid. p. 108 of Volume One.
46   Ibid. pp 287-88 of Volume One
47   Ibid. p. 89 of Volume Two.
48   Ibid. p. 221 of Volume Two.
49   Ibid. p. 150 of Volume One.
50   Ibid. p. 160 of Volume Two.
51   Ibid. p. 196 of Volume One.
52   Ibid.
53   Ibid.
54   Arthur Schopenhauer, Parerga and Paralipomena, Short Philosophical Essays, Volume 2, Oxford University Press, 1974, p. 292.
55   Arthur Schopenhauer, The World as Will and Representation, Dover Publications, New York, 1969 (two-volume edition), p. 146 of Volume One.
56   Ibid.
57   Ibid. p. 578 of Volume Two.
58   Ibid. p. 154 of Volume One.
59   Ibid. p. 354 of Volume Two.
60   Ibid. p. 147 of Volume One.
61   Arthur Schopenhauer, Parerga and Paralipomena, Short Philosophical Essays, Volume 1, Oxford University Press, 1974, p. 376.
62   Arthur Schopenhauer, Parerga and Paralipomena, Short Philosophical Essays, Volume 2, Oxford University Press, 1974, p. 296
63   Arthur Schopenhauer, The World as Will and Representation, Dover Publications, New York, 1969 (two-volume edition), p. 317 of Volume One.
64   Ibid.
65   Arthur Schopenhauer, The World as Will and Representation, Dover Publications, New York, 1969 (two-volume edition), p. 575 of Volume Two.
66   Arthur Schopenhauer, Parerga and Paralipomena, Short Philosophical Essays, Volume 2, Oxford University Press, 1974, p. 287.
67   Ibid.
68   Ibid.
69   Arthur Schopenhauer, The World as Will and Representation, Dover

Publications, New York, 1969 (two-volume edition), p. 312 of Volume One.

70 Ibid. p. 533 of Volume Two.

71 Arthur Schopenhauer, Parerga and Paralipomena, Short Philosophical Essays, Volume 2, Oxford University Press, 1974, p. 298.

72 Arthur Schopenhauer, The World as Will and Representation, Dover Publications, New York, 1969 (two-volume edition), p. 311 of Volume One

73 Arthur Schopenhauer, Parerga and Paralipomena, Short Philosophical Essays, Volume 2, Oxford University Press, 1974, p. 284.

74 Ibid. p. 298.

75 Arthur Schopenhauer, Parerga and Paralipomena, Short Philosophical Essays, Volume 1, Oxford University Press, 2015, p. 483.

76 Arthur Schopenhauer, Parerga and Paralipomena, Short Philosophical Essays, Volume 2, Oxford University Press, 1974, p. 284.

77 Ibid. p. 286.

78 Ibid. p. 287.

79 Ibid. p. 293.

80 Arthur Schopenhauer, Parerga and Paralipomena, Short Philosophical Essays, Volume 1, Cambridge University Press, 2015, Introduction.

81 Arthur Schopenhauer, The World as Will and Representation, Dover Publications, New York, 1969 (two-volume edition), p. 350 of Volume One.

82 Ibid.

83 Ibid.

84 Ibid. p. 184

85 Arthur Schopenhauer, Parerga and Paralipomena, Short Philosophical Essays, Volume 2, Oxford University Press, 1974, pp. 287-88.

86 Arthur Schopenhauer, The World as Will and Representation, Dover Publications, New York, 1969 (two-volume edition), p. 444 of Volume Two.

87 Ibid. p. 477.

88 Arthur Schopenhauer, The World as Will and Representation, Dover Publications, New York, 1969 (two-volume edition), Volume One, § 58.

89 Ibid. p. 354 of Volume Two.

90 Ibid. p. 323 of Volume One.

91 Ibid. p. 162 of Volume Two.

92 Ibid. p. 582 of Volume Two.

93   Ibid. p. 581 of Volume Two.

94   Ibid. p. 583 of Volume Two.

95   Arthur Schopenhauer, Parerga and Paralipomena, Short Philosophical Essays, Volume 2, Oxford University Press, 1974, p. 300.

96   Ibid.

97   Arthur Schopenhauer, The World as Will and Representation, Dover Publications, New York, 1969 (two-volume edition), p. 325 of Volume One.

98   Arthur Schopenhauer, Handschriftlicher Nachlass, ed. by Arthur Huebscher, Munich, 1985, Vol 3, p. 57

99   Arthur Schopenhauer, The World as Will and Representation, Dover Publications, New York, 1969 (two-volume edition), p. 357 of Volume Two.

100 Arthur Schopenhauer, Parerga and Paralipomena, Short Philosophical Essays, Volume 2, Oxford University Press, 1974, p. 604.

101 Arthur Schopenhauer, The World as Will and Representation, Dover Publications, New York, 1969 (two-volume edition), p. 354 of Volume Two.

102 Ibid. p. 372 of Volume One.

103 Arthur Schopenhauer, Prize Essay on the Basis of Morals, in The Two Fundamental Problems of Ethics, Cambridge Edition of the Works of Schopenhauer, Cambridge University Press, 2009, p. 233

104 Ibid. p. 229.

105 Ibid. p. 204.

106 Arthur Schopenhauer, The World as Will and Representation, Dover Publications, New York, 1969 (two-volume edition), p. 372 of Volume One.

107 Ibid. p. 375 ff.

108 Ibid. p. 310.

109 Arthur Schopenhauer, Prize Essay on the Basis of Morals, in The Two Fundamental Problems of Ethics, Cambridge Edition of the Works of Schopenhauer, Cambridge University Press, 2009, pp. 190-92.

110 Ibid. p. 191.

111 Arthur Schopenhauer, The World as Will and Representation, Dover Publications, New York, 1969 (two-volume edition), p. 196 of Volume One.

112 Ibid. pp. 196-97.

113 Ibid.

114 Ibid. pp. 185-86 of Volume One.

115 Ibid. p. 257 of Volume One.

116 Ibid.

117 Ibid. p. 576 of Volume Two.

118 Ibid.

119 Ibid. p. 320 of Volume One.

120 Arthur Schopenhauer, Parerga and Paralipomena, Short Philosophical Essays, Volume 2, Oxford University Press, 1974, p. 286.

121 Arthur Schopenhauer, The World as Will and Representation, Dover Publications, New York, 1969 (two-volume edition), p. 320 of Volume One.

122 Arthur Schopenhauer, Parerga and Paralipomena, Short Philosophical Essays, Volume 1, Oxford University Press, 1974, p. 336.

123 Arthur Schopenhauer, The World as Will and Representation, Dover Publications, New York, 1969 (two-volume edition), pp. 398-99 of Volume One.

124 Ibid. pp. 380-81.

125 Ibid. pp. 378-79.

126 Ibid. pp. 411-12.

127 Ibid. pp. 378-79.

128 Ibid. p. 220 of Volume One.

129 Ibid. pp. 219-220 of Volume One

130 Ibid. p. 411 of Volume One

131 Ibid. p. 374 of Volume One

132 Ibid. p. 383 of Volume One

133 Ibid. pp. 383-84.

134 Arthur Schopenhauer, Prize Essay on the Basis of Morals, in The Two Fundamental Problems of Ethics, Cambridge Edition of the Works of Schopenhauer, Cambridge University Press, 2009, p. 229.

135 Arthur Schopenhauer, The World as Will and Representation, Dover Publications, New York, 1969 (two-volume edition), pp. 326 of Volume One.

136 Ibid. p. 581 of Volume Two.

137 Arthur Schopenhauer, Parerga and Paralipomena, Short Philosophical Essays, Volume 1, Oxford University Press, 1974, p. 233.

138 Ibid. p. 477.

139 Ibid. pp. 491-92.

140 Ibid.

141 Ibid. pp. 493-94.
142 Ibid.
143 Ibid.
144 Quoted from Wolfgang Abendroth, Arthur Schopenhauer, Rowohlt Publishers, Hamburg, 1967, p. 116.
145 Arthur Schopenhauer, Parerga and Paralipomena, Short Philosophical Essays, Volume 1, Oxford University Press, 1974, p. 495.
146 Ibid. p. 288.
147 Arthur Schopenhauer, The World as Will and Representation, Dover Publications, New York, 1969 (two-volume edition), pp. 90 of Volume One.
148 Ibid. p. 345 of Volume One.
149 Ibid. p. 196 of Volume One.
150 Sigmund Freud, Future of an Illusion, in Standard Edition of the Works of Freud, Volume 21.
151 Arthur Schopenhauer, Parerga and Paralipomena, Short Philosophical Essays, Volume 2, Oxford University Press, 1974, p. 322.
152 Ibid. p. 304.
153 Ibid.
154 Ibid. p. 300.

Already published in the same series:

Walther Ziegler
Adorno in 60 Minutes
ISBN 9783750460232

Walther Ziegler
Arendt in 60 Minutes
ISBN 9783752649031

Walther Ziegler
Camus in 60 Minutes
ISBN 9783741227738

Walther Ziegler
Confucius in 60 Minutes
ISBN 9783753423128

Walther Ziegler
Foucault in 60 Minutes
ISBN 978375342688

Walther Ziegler
Freud in 60 Minutes
ISBN 9783741227707

Walther Ziegler
Habermas in 60 Minutes
ISBN 9783752612370

Walther Ziegler
Hegel in 60 Minutes
ISBN 9783741227677

Walther Ziegler
Heidegger in 60 Minutes
ISBN 9783741227752

Walther Ziegler
Hobbes in 60 Minutes
ISBN 9783751968317

Walther Ziegler
Kant in 60 Minutes
ISBN 9783741226373

Walther Ziegler
Marx in 60 Minutes
ISBN 9783741227691

Walther Ziegler
Nietzsche in 60 Minutes
ISBN 9783752803822

Walther Ziegler
Rawls in 60 Minutes
ISBN 9783750424050

Walther Ziegler
Rousseau in 60 Minutes
ISBN 9783741227622

Walther Ziegler
Sartre in 60 Minutes
ISBN 9783741227653

Walther Ziegler
Smith in 60 Minutes
ISBN 9783741227721

Walther Ziegler
Platon in 60 Minutes
ISBN 9783741227615

Walther Ziegler
Popper in 60 Minutes
ISBN 9783750470897

Walther Ziegler
Schopenhauer in 60 Minutes
ISBN 9783750498853

Walther Ziegler
Wittgenstein in 60 Minutes
ISBN 9783750426955

The author:

Dr Walther Ziegler is academically trained in the fields of philosophy, history and political science. As a foreign correspondent, reporter and newsroom coordinator for the German TV station ProSieben he has produced films on every continent. His news reports have won several prizes and awards. He has also authored numerous books in the field of philosophy. His many years of experience as a journalist mean that he is able to present the complex ideas of the great philosophers in a way that is both engaging and very clear. Since 2007 he has also been active as a teacher and trainer of young TV journalists in Munich, holding the post of Academic Director at the Media Academy, a University of Applied Sciences that offers film and TV courses at its base directly on the site of the major European film production company Bavaria Film. After the huge success of the book series "Great thinkers in 60 Minutes", he works as a freelance writer and philosopher.